Travelling by Train in the 'Twenties and 'Thirties

Travelling by Train
in the 'Twenties and 'Thirties

Philip Unwin

London
GEORGE ALLEN & UNWIN
Boston   Sydney

First published in 1981

GEORGE ALLEN & UNWIN LTD
40 Museum Street, London WC1A 1LU

© George Allen & Unwin (Publishers) Ltd, 1981

British Library Cataloguing in Publication Data

Unwin, Philip
    Travelling by train in the twenties and thirties.
    1. Railroads – Great Britain – History
    I. Title
    385'.0941   HE3018

    ISBN 0–04–385086–3

Picture research by Mike Esau

Set in 10/12 point Bembo by Nene Phototypesetters Ltd
and printed in Great Britain
by Biddles Ltd, Guildford, Surrey.

Contents

Illustrations

Acknowledgements

I must offer my warm thanks to Professor Jack Simmons both for the encouragement I have received from him for the idea of attempting to write this book and his care in reading the typescript, also for giving me the great benefit of his comments.

I am also in debt to Mike Esau for his ingenuity and skill in discovering exactly the photographs I wanted to illustrate the locomotives, the rolling stock and the general scenes of the period; while the works of Hamilton Ellis, O. S. Nock, C. F. Klapper and back numbers of the *Railway Magazine* have again proved invaluable for reference.

P.U.

Introduction

A *Punch* cartoon of 60 years ago showed a very Victorian-looking locomotive, covered with cobwebs, and stationary on a level crossing because of the railway strike declared by the NUR and supported by the ASLEF, though the latter had no grievance at that time. On the road was a lorry from which the friendly driver was offering a lift to a girl. The comment from the unhappy looking engine was 'Once aboard the lorry, and the girl is mine – no more' – the cartoonist had already designated her as 'the Goods'. It seemed a harmless *Punch* joke at the time but it pointed to enormous future problems for railways.

That strike of 1919, too, was a threat. It was a protest against the proposal that the lower grades of railwaymen should take a cut in their wages as costs of living were then declining from their war-time level, but such a strike had been unknown since 1911. 'Anything to beat the strikers' became the cry as volunteers flocked to offer their services to the railways. Anyone qualified to act as crew upon an engine was specially welcome and there seems to have been no serious picketing.

Describing his experiences in the *Railway Magazine* a volunteer fireman on the GWR wrote of quickly getting accustomed to 'putting one in each corner and one in the middle' (shovelfuls in the firebox) then finishing up at Old Oak Common for the night. There, in a siding, was a train of old compartment stock with a rug and pillow for each man and a tank engine in steam at the head to provide heating. The morning call came at 5 a.m. and there were worse breakfasts than a hunk of bread and margarine – butter still rationed – with a thick slice of fat bacon and tea. The writer was working on slow trains out to Reading and back. A nice old lady tipped him a shilling at Paddington one day while a first class gentleman complained that the train was five minutes late! Though they were trying to work to an emergency timetable it inevitably took longer than usual at each station as passengers hunted for seats, then

THE DELIVERER.

LOCOMOTIVE (*stationary through strike*). "ONCE ABOARD THE LORRY AND THE GIRL IS MINE
—NO MORE!"

Punch

1. 'The Deliverer', *Punch's* view of the 1919 railway strike when, for the first time, with hundreds of
ex-Army lorries being sold off cheaply and their former drivers being demobilised from the Forces,
railways faced serious competition. No longer were they the only means of distributing goods on a
large scale.

had to squeeze in somehow. Nineteen in one third class compartment was considered a good load.

At some points the volunteer engine crews were cheered by passengers and frequently a collection was made for them on the train; at others there might be a group of booing strikers some of whom hurled balls of screwed-up paper at the engine cab, but no injury resulted from such antics. It appears to have been a good humoured affair in the main but inconvenience to the travelling public was intense. The Lancashire and Yorkshire Railway, proudly known as 'the business line' had 98 per cent of its operating staff on strike. Nevertheless they managed to run over 200 trains in a week (no Sundays) and details of the emergency timetable were circulated to post offices, newspapers, hotels and clubs. Over 400 volunteers did platform duties, acted as assistant guards and firemen, the latter under the supervision of 'loyal men and inspectors'. Livestock in transit at the start of the strike were kept fed and watered while the Conference Room at the Company's Manchester headquarters was turned into a vast dormitory for the volunteers. Over the country some 4,000 trains ran on the Saturday where but 600 ran on the first day of the strike. The following week it was called off on a promise that the proposed cuts in wages should be postponed.

With so few owning cars at the time and the great bulk of goods being carried by rail, the strike could soon have had serious effects. It did however show up the enthusiasm of young men to have a go at railway work and it prepared the way for similar resistance, seven years later, to the General Strike.

It must be recorded also, that volunteers spoke of having received 'every courtesy from the Inspectors and the Shed Foremen'. There seemed at that time little of the bitterness which later entered into Union relationships. One signalman at an important box on the LSWR, some way from the nearest station, thoughtfully warned the young Special Constable who was on guard there that, should he have a call of nature, he must under no circumstances 'do it on the conductor rail'.

With the decade of the 1920s, railway conditions began steadily to improve and led on to some of the greatest progress we had ever seen; the aim of this book is to describe its main features and to record how some of it seemed at the time.

I
The Grouping

'Through Carriage Aberdeen to Penzance' was one of the more sensational railway announcements of 1921. It could not have concerned more than a tiny fraction of the travelling public but it stood for several important and interesting things. First it showed that after a total of seven years of war and its aftermath under the control of the Government, the railways at last had a chance to show some enterprise again. Secondly, it was a reminder of the greater amount of co-operation which could be achieved by the leading railways of the country. Consideration of some form of amalgamation, even nationalisation, was much in the air at the time because the unified control under the Railways Executive Committee had shown great advantages in the special conditions of wartime working.

Meanwhile, that Great Western, or North Eastern, coach with the enormous destination board inscribed ABERDEEN–PENZANCE via EDINBURGH YORK SHEFFIELD LEICESTER SWINDON AND PLYMOUTH must have made a big impression wherever it stopped. The particular lines involved were the Caledonian, North British, North Eastern, Great Central and Great Western. What a prospect for the truly dedicated buff! Any hero who made the entire journey southbound would have been on the move from Aberdeen 9.45 a.m. to Penzance at 7.40 the next morning and the going in the reverse direction

was similar in its timing. Average speed was little more than 30 mph and a good deal of time must have been spent with that coach standing in stations waiting for the next connection. A quicker journey via London (King's Cross and Paddington) was doubtless possible but that is not the point. Many living in the North and Midlands would have benefited from some part of the journey and anyhow it made good railway publicity. In a sense it was one stepping stone on the way to the Grouping which was to come very shortly.

There was something ridiculous about a country the size of Great Britain having over 120 private railway companies. Some of them were very small but at least 20 were substantial undertakings, each with its own works for the building of its own rolling stock. Most had their own individual livery and had to deal separately with the mass of intricate detail which goes into the running of a railway. After the experience of the 1914 War it was obvious to many that some degree of amalgamation was essential but the form it was to take became an anxiety to passengers and railway staff alike. Some of the financially weak and less efficient were expected to gain but would there be a pulling down of the standards of the better and more popular lines? The idea of the 'Big Four' Groups serving roughly, the north, east, south and west of the country, as evolved by the companies them-

1

2. The 'Continental' appearance of this short stove-pipe chimney originated with R. W. Urie's later design of 4–6–0 on the LSWR. No. 476 was one of a later batch of mixed traffic two-cylinder engines actually built in the time of R. E. Maunsell in early Southern days. Here it is shown on the important 'up milk' service, near Raynes Park, bringing milk into the metropolitan area from the West Country. Having run at express speeds earlier, it now slopes along on the slow road, about to stop and unload its churns at Wimbledon and Clapham. The varied rolling stock includes four, six and eight-wheeled vans from LSWR, LBSCR and the SECR.

selves, under Government pressure, proved eminently sound. So came about the London Midland and Scottish, the London and North Eastern, the Southern and the Great Western. No one wanted to disturb the main lines and the traffic they handled but it was essential to reduce overlapping and unnecessary competition. In Victorian days of unbridled enterprise many a small town was served by two separate lines, each with its own station. They were often pretty little buildings, properly staffed and equipped with signal-box and sidings but with minimal traffic and that likely to disappear

within a few years. One was sad to see them go but it was quite inevitable.

The Grouping took effect on 1 January 1923 and one looked anxiously for any immediate sign of it. After a month or so there was at Waterloo a printed notice – of a statutory kind relating to freight rates (of no interest to passengers) but it *was* headed SOUTHERN RAILWAY. Then came other pieces of printed matter which had the same magic words in bold type before retreating into 'London and South Western Section' below it. After some six months there were electric trains appearing with

2

3. The largest engine of the former LBSCR, the 4–6–4 two-cylinder class express tank loco, later re-built by Maunsell as a tender engine. No. B330 has emerged from Merstham tunnel, with what appears to be a Brighton excursion judging by the special number board on the front. The stock is mainly that of the LSWR, a somewhat scratch lot – some with the very low roof which denotes the 1880s. Scarcely any one has a lavatory: the year is 1926.

SOUTHERN emblazoned upon the narrow panel above the windows of the carriages instead of the former arrangement of LSWR at the waist-line. Next came the impressive moment of see-ing the word actually on an engine; at first merely on the side of an 0–4–4 tank but then right across the tender of a Urie 4–6–0 with a little letter 'E' below it (to show that it was an Eastleigh engine) and below that, the number of the locomotive in huge figures. This latter style had been practised by the Midland but it was dropped in LMS days in favour of the initials which remained right up to nationalisation.

This matter of liveries for the new Groups was an intense interest to regular travellers and to all enthusiasts. On the whole the decisions made worked quite well but it was of course im-possible to please everybody. The much ad-mired 'Derby red' of the Midland became the colour for both carriages and locomotives of the vast LMS until the financial stringencies of the 1930s forced them to go over to black for most of their engines. Yet that colour which looked so rich when the Midland could afford to keep it immaculately clean and to apply no less than seventeen coats of paint and varnish to its carriages, somehow never seemed to suit the rather skinny looking LNWR coaches (though

4. The all-Pullman 'Southern Belle', steam-hauled in LBSCR days. The I3 class 4–4–2 tank engine was a comparatively early and highly successful example of superheating. When occasionally working on a through train from Brighton to Rugby it so impressed the LNWR authorities by its efficiency and fuel economy that it led in the early 1900s to the wide adoption of superheating by Crewe and to the building of the famous George V class of 4–4–0s.

they were extremely well-built and stood up to minor accidents much better than their glossier Midland counterparts). There was too, the loss of the famous 'plum and spilt milk' livery which, combined with the blackberry black of the engines had always been a characteristic of the North Western. No, one had some sympathy for the Euston regulars.

On the LNER travellers on the famous East Coast route still had their handsome green engines and teak carriages of the Great Northern but NER enthusiasts must have regretted the passing of their plum-red carriages. Across the Border the distinctive brownish-green of the North British engines was missed as they went into the bright green of the LNER. Curiously

enough the blue which British Rail finally adopted so enthusiastically, was the one colour which almost completely disappeared under Grouping (apart from the Somerset & Dorset Joint Railway). The fine ultramarine blue of the GER locomotives with their vermilion lining-out and coupling rods – the best part of a rather dingy railway – went, as did the handsome all-blue engines of the Caledonian. In the latter case it was the widely embracing Derby red which covered them and again, did not seem to suit the Scottish locomotives particularly well.

Now to take the Groups individually let us consider first the Southern. Although the smallest, with a total route mileage of but 2,200 (compared with the 7,790 miles of the LMS), it had three distinct sides: first, the most intensive suburban system in the world set in the prosperous south-east corner of Britain; second, the whole southern coast with all its resorts, as far west as Exmouth, as well as part of the north Cornish and Devon coast; and lastly, the cross-Channel steamer services. It was responsible for the major part of all traffic to the Continent and it had thus borne a quite exceptional extra load throughout the war and was correspondingly worn down.

One of the Group's greatest assets lay in Sir Herbert Walker, KCB. Tall, imposing and the type of man for whom colleagues stood up instinctively when he entered the board room, he was one of the wisest and most successful railway managers of this century. Gifted with an acute financial mind and one which instantly recalled the technical details – platforms, sidings and signalling – of any station which he had inspected, he had a brilliant career on the old LNWR. However, in spite of having appeared for them most effectively at many inquiries, he had, at 43, been advanced only to Outdoor Goods Manager while effectively acting as Assistant General Manager. Dissatisfied by his prospects at Euston he accepted in 1912 the invitation to become the General Manager for the LSWR at Waterloo. Already a marked man, he became chairman of the Railways Executive Committee through which the Government controlled the railways throughout the 1914 war. With such a career behind him he was the obvious choice as General Manager for the Southern in 1923. He had, moreover, unflappable qualities and a strength of constitution which had enabled him to spend long tedious days at Westminster on the Railways Executive Committee during the war, when he was also running the LSWR at its most testing time. It was fortunate indeed for the Southern that in 1923 Walker was in his prime and well able to

face the complications and the entirely new set of problems involved in the building up of a successful Group at a time of changing travel patterns, motor car competition and ever rising costs.

By 1922 the enormous work of rebuilding Waterloo station had been completed. After the complicated muddle of the earlier structure it became with its 21 platforms the largest, as well as the lightest, cleanest looking and best sign-posted of any London terminus with all its platforms ending neatly in line with their magnificent Ransome and Rapier hydraulic buffers which shot a neat squirt of water up to the roof when an engine had once run gently into them. In fact one never heard of LSWR drivers hitting the buffers – it seemed to be Euston where that happened, after the great descent of the Camden Bank. There was also a very fine block of offices which housed much of the new Group's administration. Walker himself, though he had pushed forward completion of the new station and was a keen advocate of electrification, inhabited a handsome room in the surviving block of the old station on the York Road, and he insisted on having a good coal fire in it!

For all its heavy wartime burdens the LSWR was in fair shape by 1923 with a number of new engines and many more rebuilt. A good and economical start had been made with suburban electrification and there was more to come. But much the most pressing problems were on the SECR which still suffered from the inherent weaknesses of the original London, Chatham and Dover. That line, much lampooned in the past, had continued to run to some extent in direct competition with the South Eastern, although both were controlled by a Managing Committee from 1899 onwards. Each still had its separate routes to the Channel ports and their continental traffic was worked into different

London termini, the LC & D routes into Victoria, the SECR into Charing Cross. The under-bridge work was weak and their lines could not bear the weight of a 4–6–0 engine. One cannot forget the sight of an important supporting pier from the old bridge over the LSWR main line at Queens Road, Battersea, after it was laid beside the track when new steel ones were fitted in early Southern days. The old LC & D pier had been a good imitation Doric column with fluted sides, but it was now revealed to be quite hollow and made of cast iron. Similar problems had to be sorted out in many parts of the important London to Dover line before the increasingly heavy continental boat trains could be drawn by the size of engine they needed. Meanwhile, for the first few years of the Southern such trains had to be double-headed, frequently by Drummond T9s borrowed from the western section.

The SECR suburban lines were another pressing problem. Six days a week they carried some of the heaviest commuter traffic in the world in rather awful six-, and often four-wheeled carriages, and these so narrow that you were apt to rub knees with the traveller opposite. The aim was, of course, to electrify these lines – it should have been done before the war but the Management Committee had lacked both cash and the necessary drive. The LBSCR was in rather better condition, having done a useful piece of inner suburban electrification, between Victoria and London Bridge in 1909. However, this was on the 6,600-volt overhead alternating system which could not be married to the LSWR 600-volt direct which had served the Thames Valley area well since 1915. For the rest, the steam services to Brighton and the coast were quite respectable though the line had never risen to corridor coaches. It was in need of modernisation yet it did have an enviable reputation for the smooth running of its eight-wheel bogie stock

with its curiously low roofs (some of these later found their way on to the western section as 'trailer' coaches for the three-coach electric units and were noticeably smoother at speed than the indigenous vehicles).

Altogether there was a tremendous programme to be tackled, not only to remedy serious defects, but also to evolve a well co-ordinated railway service for the south of England which would be able to meet road competition. Though steam is our primary subject, and Herbert Walker did not neglect it, one must pay tribute to the tremendous march he stole upon the other three Groups in his determination to press electrification. In 1923 he could claim that where the LSWR carried 500,000 passengers p.a. on the Thames Valley lines in 1915 under steam, they now carried over 1,000,000 with electrification in the same area. In another twelve years he would be showing how on the Bexleyheath and Sidcup line (of the old SECR) passengers had risen from 1,000,000 to 4,800,000 p.a., and a threefold increase had come on the Epsom Downs branch of the LBSC.

These results owed much, of course, to the great increase in house building which developed alongside the lines which offered such an improved service. Also, the regular interval timetable which Walker insisted upon – trains for a given route leaving the terminus at the same number of minutes past the hour – saved looking up a timetable and made the suburban journey as simple as catching a tram or bus. This principle was extended to main line trains and, from Waterloo, expresses left for Exeter and Plymouth on the hour every two hours up to 3 p.m. and then 6 p.m.; to Bournemouth hourly at the half hour; and to Portsmouth at 50 minutes past the hour. For the most part the slower trains likewise ran at regular times past the hour.

The summer of 1924 was the nadir of the

5. A GWR two-cylinder Saint class 4–6–0 near Shrewsbury with a remarkable assortment of rolling stock including LNWR in old livery followed by a narrow LNWR coach in LMS colours, then mainly GWR with the exception of the dining car which appears to be a clerestoried LNWR twelve-wheeler. Such variety was common in the 'twenties, especially where LMS and GWR met.

Southern in the public estimation. Great engineering works of all kinds were going ahead: bridges rebuilt, track relaid, and conductor rails with all the attendant complications of electrification were installed. New engines were being planned, but meanwhile the motive power position was definitely under strength and it was difficult, frequently, to keep time.

On many a journey one encountered the temporary line-side board, arrow pointed at one end and a red lamp set in it to warn of a coming speed slack. The brakes sighed on, then there was the next warning of the large illuminated letter C for Commencement of the slow section, which you traversed at about 15 mph until you reached the sign of T indicating Termination, and you then picked up speed again. Inevitably, train after

train was delayed and passenger discontent was further inflamed because many of the coaches, especially on the SECR, were very old and the better ones were in the workshops being rebuilt on to bogie under-frames and adapted for electric working. Protesting letters to the Press multiplied and during the silly season of that year the *Daily Express* conceived the idea of a stunt attacking the Southern Railway. Almost daily a funny article appeared under the name of 'Luke Speedwell' in which the most was made of every single mishap and delay which had occurred. It was said that reporters were sent to Victoria and Charing Cross each morning in search of 'stories' from incoming travellers.

In the middle of it all Sir Herbert Walker was on a short continental holiday and on his return

6. The classic GNR Atlantic 4–4–2, designed by Ivatt in 1902 and now shown in LNER livery in 1925. This type was the mainstay of the Anglo-Scottish East Coast service south of York for over twenty years and is here seen starting from King's Cross with a Leeds and Harrogate express. The second and third coaches are specimens of the handsome Edwardian twelve-wheeled clerestory corridor coaches once famous on the Scotch Expresses.

to Folkestone he was mobbed by reporters who pursued him to his reserved seat in the Pullman car of the boat train where tea and toast was served. Very wisely he refused to be drawn into any comment on the Southern at that stage: 'I cannot say a word' was all they got out of him.

It was not long, however, before he secured the services of John Elliot, an able and successful Fleet Street man who became the first PRO ever to be employed by a railway (though not so designated then). He gained the complete confidence of the Chairman and all the plans for the regeneration of the railway and the progress of the work were disclosed to Elliot. Within a comparatively short time he produced a well-informed and interesting article entitled 'The

Truth About the Southern'. After spelling out the tremendous contribution of its three lines to the war effort of 1914 to 1918 and the price that had been paid in worn out track and rolling stock, Elliot went on to describe the massive works now in hand including, of course, the electrification on the SECR and further parts of the LBSCR, and the new express engines, corridor carriages and restaurant cars to come. Other authoritative articles followed, so attractively written that editors readily published them and in no time the hitherto disgruntled travellers had a very different talking point. Sir John Elliot, as he became, did great work for the Southern and finished up as its Chairman.

In the summer of the following year, 1925,

7. Exquisitely clean ex-GNR Atlantic takes this Newmarket race special from King's Cross, via the Cambridge line, in April 1925. She contrasts strangely with the rather dowdy-looking train of straight-sided Pullmans which were gathered up for the occasion from the Southern. They were originally used by the SECR and are still painted in their former crimson lake.

posters appeared, well designed and printed in several colours, listing the principal details of the Southern resurgence and the money spent on them. A leading item was the number of new express passenger engines being built, the new carriages and the miles of track being relaid. It was all most impressive especially as these good things, including some of the King Arthur class 4–6–0 locomotives, began to go into service. The naming of the new engines after the heroes of the Arthurian legend was another of Elliot's ideas and most appropriate for the line serving the Tintagel area – even if none of them worked beyond Exeter.

Herbert Walker was one of our greatest railwaymen but he had no personal sense of pub-licity: his concern was to take the right decisions then to give every encouragement to those he had selected to do the job. It was typical of him to make no advance public announcement about the new escalator at Waterloo which was to lift Underground passengers right up to the level of the circulating area of the main station. Just one day the surrounding boards and dust sheets were removed and there was the double escalator (with a flight of fixed stairs between for those nervous of the 'moving stairs' – as they were called, then still a rarity), an enormous convenience for those who had already trudged up from the Waterloo and City line unkindly known as the 'Drain'. More will be said later of the engine, rolling stock and ship achievements

8. LNER (ex-North London Railway) suburban travel in its plainest form in the 1920s. The twelve coaches are all four-wheelers and the greatest care was taken to ensure that no-one should put his head out of the double-barred windows. The provision of a whole coach at each end of the train for luggage seems excessive. The little 4–4–0 tank locomotive is similar to that used on the Metropolitan Underground lines in their steam-worked days.

of the Southern, but this gives some idea of the difficulties which had to be faced before it could develop into a line offering the highest *all-round* standards of comfort and punctuality in the country.

By contrast, the next Group in size, the Great Western with over 3,700 miles was much less of a problem and its development was comparatively straightforward. It had been the greatest, and one of the more profitable of the pre-war lines and the news that it was to retain its identity gave enormous satisfaction to its supporters; it was the only line to do so and its personality lived on to nationalisation in 1948. It had bought up the smaller Welsh railways such as the Cambrian and the Barry, and those of the South Wales Docks in 1922, so it was ideally placed to control everything in Wales apart from the north coast and one or two other points where the LMS appeared. It had not been obliged to bear the enormous extra loads of wartime traffic on the same scale as the Southern, the magnificent engines of G. J. Churchward were still well able to cope with the traffic and they did not have the legacy of poor track and badly out-dated equipment which afflicted parts of the Southern.

It was still the fact that in out of the way parts of the system you might encounter rather appalling local trains with very ancient and hard riding six-wheelers though they were hauled by good 4–4–0 locomotives sometimes even by a 4–6–0, but on the whole the main line services were at a high standard.

Then there was the great event of C. B. Collett's first post-war engine 'Caerphilly Castle'. A development from Churchward's Star class, O. S. Nock has stated that 'It is no exaggeration to say that the Castle is one of the most famous and successful designs the world has ever seen' and he pointed out that they were built unchanged from 1923 to 1939. Even after the last war they were still being made with only minor modifications up to 1950. They were four cylinder and of somewhat complicated interior design which called for skilled workshop handling in their maintenance and repair. They did not fulfil the Urie aim for 'everything get-atable' but the Castles were exceptional for power and speed and general economy in running. By odd chance I was hauled by 'Pendennis Castle' from Newton Abbot to Exeter in 1924 when she was new and I saw her again at Didcot on her last journey to Southampton in 1977 before she was shipped to Australia. There was something enormously satisfying in the design with those huge steam pipes curving down from smokebox to the cylinders. Other modern 4–6–0s such as the King Arthurs had them but they were straight and were partly covered up by smoke deflectors. These latter the GWR never had to use because their tapering boilers left enough space at the front end for a chimney of decent height (to carry away the smoke properly). Side-view also they looked 'just right' – coupled wheels well spaced out and not cramped together like some designs which strove to reduce the overall length of the engine. More will be said about GWR engines in our chapter on loco-

motives, suffice it to say here that of all the Groups that line was the most advanced in 1923 and it underwent no period of inadequate motive power, or uncertainty over the precise types of engine to be built. The new ones which appeared followed GWR tradition and there were no sensational changes.

There had to be no major alteration in top management. Both Sir James Milne and Sir Felix J. Pole, who cover our period, were GWR men through and through, the latter having served the line for thirty years and the former some twenty years. Thus the fine traditions of the GWR continued but with undoubted conservatism which at times had an almost Victorian flavour to it. Those handsome funnels with their copper rims at the top and certain of the carriages with their clerestory roofs and right-angle-shaped side handles were unmistakable. Supporters of the GWR had an unanswerable point to make when argument arose in youthful circles on the merits of the various lines: 'It was the only one to become a Group on its own and to retain its name and identity'.

Like the Southern it became very clever at the establishment of an effective Publicity Department. Their issue of three admirably produced paperbacks – 'For Boys of all Ages' – well illustrated, printed on art paper and entitled *The 10.30 Limited*, *Caerphilly Castle* and *Brunel and After* was a master stroke. Issued at only one shilling each, the first sold 40,000 in its first month and all of them left the reader with the impression that the GWR was *the* outstanding line. Its reputation for high speeds was wonderfully burnished by the introduction in 1923 of the so-called 'Cheltenham Flyer' a train which, after a slow progress through Gloucester and Stroud, was run non-stop from Swindon to Paddington. Swindon station platform stands a little higher than the cross at the top of St Paul's Cathedral so the run to Paddington is comparatively easy; and with no busy suburban approach an average of just over 60 mph with a fairly light load is no great feat, 77 miles in 75 minutes. Then it was done in 70 minutes and in 1932 in 65 minutes making an average speed of 71·4 mph. The Press was kept well informed and on a day when a particularly fast run was expected reporters would be on the platform and good stories would appear the next day. So what at first was the 'Fastest Train in the Kingdom' became 'in the British Empire' and finally 'in the World' – that is, as a regularly scheduled run. Part of the charm lay in the fact that the original train, in the words of Hamilton Ellis 'looked like a perfectly ordinary Great Western express: some of the carriages were ancient, and the engine a fair veteran' (the two-cylinder 'Saint Bartholomew', c.1904). In other words, it was a typical specimen of GWR everyday service. How many of the sober residents of Cheltenham actually patronised the train is not known, but that dashing run from Swindon became a famous piece of publicity for the railway.

Meanwhile the GWR advanced steadily on its three trunk routes: to the West country, to South Wales and the Birmingham and Birkenhead line. It had been a well managed system and it could be said that the Grouping made little difference to it. It continued to go its own way successfully, and advanced further in locomotive design with the King class 4–6–0 engines.

The second largest of the newly created Groups was the London and North Eastern which embraced the constituent parts of the so-called East Coast route to Scotland, namely the Great Northern, the North Eastern, the North British and the Great North of Scotland, plus the Great Central and the Great Eastern. The Hull and Barnsley had been acquired by the NER in 1922. It had the worst inheritance, financially, of all the Groups. The GCR (London extension) never paid and should never

have been built though it was most pleasant to travel upon. The GER with little freight and thinly populated country was financially weak; the NBR was rickety after a costly and fully justified dispute with the Government over wartime compensation.

The Group had a total mileage of 6,590 and, curiously, the first three lines mentioned above all depended upon the 4–4–2 Atlantic-type locomotive for their main passenger services (though the GNR and NER had experimented with one type of 4–6–2 Pacific). All the 4–4–2s were comparatively small engines compared to the GWR 4–6–0s but they were thoroughly effective at the time and lasted until many more of Gresley's Pacifics could take to the road. Doncaster was the headquarters of the Group, its works for the production of locos and rolling stock were directed by Nigel Gresley, a Great Northern man, later to be knighted. The General Manager was Ralph Wedgwood, of the North Eastern, and between them they created a fine railway with a strong flavour of the GNR. The LNER came deservedly to the fore in 1935 with the streamlined 'Silver Jubilee' non-stop express between Kings Cross and Newcastle-upon-Tyne which averaged 70 mph most of the way and frequently exceeded 100 mph. In 1937, in honour of the coronation of King George VI, there was a similar train, London to Edinburgh with one stop at York doing the entire journey in six hours. These performances were made possible by Gresley's refinements to his original Pacific design, then known as the 'A4'. They were the fastest booked regular steam runs anywhere.

It was noticeable, too, how the GER section seemed to advance under it and on a train from Liverpool Street station one would suddenly come upon some Great Northern corridor carriages – of pre-1914 vintage but likely to be more comfortable than their GER predecessors.

9. The eternal Webb Precedent class 2–4–0, introduced as a type by the LNWR in 1874, seen leaving Carlisle for Penrith in 1930 boldly lettered LMS (but probably painted black). Except that the coaches are in the LMS maroon, the train is pure 'Nor' Western' – the leading coach a comfortable lavatory composite eight-wheeler and further back some six-wheelers.

By that time Kings Cross was enjoying the comfort of Gresley's ingenious articulated sets of five coaches mounted on only six bogies. Though the severe trade depression of the 1930s was to hit the heavy industries of the north-east of England seriously and reduce the traffic of the LNER it remained a well managed Group efficient in goods, passenger and shipping services.

The LMS in its origins was exceptionally difficult. It embraced the LNWR, Midland, North Staffordshire, Lancashire & Yorkshire, Furness, Caledonian, Glasgow & South Western and Highland Railways. With its great mileage of 7,790 it was the largest of the Big Four sprawling out to part of South Wales, North Wales, and even Southend, as well as the vast mass of the Midlands and North West and much

13

of Scotland. Its two main parts the LNWR and the Midland Railway were proud and powerful, worked in different ways, had their jealousies and weaknesses and were greatly in need of strong and gifted management. The Group seemed to have bad luck in its early years and it was said that it was 'too big' to function successfully. Sir Guy Granet, Chairman of the Midland since 1906, had assumed leadership of the LMS but with his retirement in view he sought, in the words of Hamilton Ellis 'a potential dictator' and found him in the brilliant, genial but completely tough Sir Josiah Stamp who became, in 1926, President of the Executive, then General Manager and finally Chairman. Though no railwayman, he was a great economist and administrator and proved to be exactly the new mind which was so badly needed for the Group's affairs. It was his insistence – from the top – that a fuller and faster service must be run by 1927 and that locomotives of ample power must be produced, which resulted in the 'Royal Scot' 4–6–0s. Previously, there had been deadlock over the rival plans of Crewe and Derby. The details are given in the next chapter.

Following the successful debut of the Scots with their regular non-stop runs of 299 miles from London to Carlisle, beating the 226 miles of the 'Cornish Riviera' to Plymouth, there were smaller but additional 4–6–0 engines such as the Patriots (the so-called 'Baby Scots').

The introduction of new carriages added interesting variety to the typical LMS express from Euston. There was still much of the old LNWR wooden corridor stock to be seen – actually one could meet it as far off as Plymouth on some through trains from the north – it was short and narrow with a flattish roof and no hint of a clerestory. Its plum and spilt milk livery was to be seen for some years and it inclined to look all wrong when it was repainted in Midland colours. All the new stock was higher and wider, as had been the case with the best of the LNWR carriages. The new LMS carriages looked altogether bigger and they indicated only three-a-side in a corridor compartment by providing two folding arms to support the passenger in the middle seat. Another variety was the quite frequent appearance of an MR clerestory coach on the old LNWR trains so that on one of them you might see the three distinct sorts of carriage and the near raspberry and cream effect of the colours of the two original companies!

The dining car services like the hotels of the Midland were always excellent under the care of the Towle family, Sir William and then his sons, and their influence seemed to permeate the LMS. The first train journey I made in 1932 as a newly married man was from Euston to Rugby preparatory to going on to Windermere next day for the honeymoon. After the tensions of the ceremony and the reception, on a five o'clock train nothing seemed more welcome than freshly made tea and toast. I never forgot the pretty tea set decorated with pink roses and the charming steward – observing the smiling couple, new clothes and brand new luggage – who offered to serve it in the compartment (first class for that section of the journey!). With a nice clean old Claughton at the head of the train what more could one want, and I was only gently admonished for my ungallantry in leaving my bride unattended for a few moments while I ran up to the front of the train to inspect the engine. For all I knew it could have been one of so many different types in those days. Tea the next day, in a fine new twelve-wheeled restaurant car was equally good, and again served with pink roses. We anticipated it once more on our return journey when our through coaches from Windermere were supposed to be attached to the up Irish Mail at Crewe. Alas, we went adrift in some way, being held up in the yard, while that famous train, headed by a Scot, thundered past us into the station and was well on its way by the time we crept into the platform. We became a three-coach relief train drawn by an old Precursor and our tea was served in plain white cups from a trolley on the station platform. (At least they had saucers and were not made of plastic.)

By the early 1930s one could see a very fine railway taking shape in the LMS and there were good opportunities to observe it at close range if one had business regularly at Euston. Into one short-bay platform, near to the old Underground entrance, they used to shunt – presumably for the inspection of High Officials – a specimen of each one of the new types of carriages as they were turned out from the works at Wolverton. So, from platform level one could scrutinise the newest third class corridor coach with the aforesaid arms and provision for only three-a-side; first class ditto. Then, some weeks later, a 12-wheeler dining car would appear and after that a sleeper and here the third class could be of special interest to many because they had been introduced only a year or two back.

Then there was the time in 1933 when the successor to the Royal Scots was to be seen, the mighty Pacific, the 'Princess Royal'. At about 6 p.m. one had a good chance of seeing her at the end of her run on the up Royal Scot express. She was an enormously impressive engine, looking more massive than the LNER Pacifics and by comparison with the LMS in the 1920s one felt that the Group had really arrived – at least so far as its best long distance services were concerned.

2
Locomotives

From the time of the Grouping there was naturally a tendency to reduce the number of former types, but in the 1920s there was still an astonishing profusion of them to be seen. It became an interesting exercise to identify the older locos in their new colours – an old LNWR Precursor, perhaps, in the new LMS colours, or a GER Holden 4–4–0 repainted from its lovely blue to look like a sort of GNR engine in the colours of the new LNER, or again an LBSCR taken out of its rather unique brown livery and put into Southern green. A visit to some of the London termini could give one a remarkable view of thirty years of locomotive design plus the new types which were appearing.

To take Kings Cross, first and foremost there was the immensely exciting spectacle of the first post-war Pacific. True there had been 'The Great Bear' in 1908 but she was confined to the GWR London to Bristol run and apart from her extra length and the trailing wheel below her firebox she did not look – to a boy – so very different from a Star. The 'Great Northern', however, built in 1922, looked altogether different – huge and very graceful compared to the Atlantics which still did most of the hard passenger work. There were also Gresley's excellent new 2–6–0s which had preceded them and pioneered his ingenious rocking shaft arrangement by which the one inside cylinder valve was actuated by levers connected with the valve gear of the two outside cylinders. There were, too, the older 4–4–0s, very nippy on semi-fast trains, and there were powerful 0–6–2 tank engines which handled the suburban trains very efficiently. To see any express engine leave King's Cross on a train then had a certain dash about it. At the end of the platform it appeared to dive down at once below the platform level in order to get into Copenhagen Tunnel which, of course, had to be low enough to allow the railway to pass under the Regent's Canal and then begin that stiff climb, through the always damp and smoky tunnel. With a platform engine banking the train out, it made a smart get-away but it was a hard start to a journey. Some years later, a father often meeting his St Andrews University daughter off the 'Flying Scotsman' could admire the magnificence of the Pacific as she shot up from that tunnel, straightened herself out and, entering that long, straight platform remarkably fast, made a very fine journey's end. (I had a good view because the Dundee coaches were always at the rear.)

Those Gresley Pacifics were said to inaugurate an altogether new era of the steam locomotive. They did not come to their full fruition (in the streamlined engines of the 'Silver Jubilee' high speed express) until the refinements of some years later but as a design they were a long way ahead of most Edwardian locomotives which had seemed good in their way but which could

GREAT WESTERN "KING" CLASS OF LOCOMOTIVES COMPARED WITH OTHER LARGE EXPRESS BRITISH LOCOMOTIVES. TO THE SAME SCALE.

LOCOMOTIVE.	WEIGHT.	TRACTIVE EFFORT.
G.W.R. "KING" CLASS. 4-6-0 TYPE.	TONS. CWTS. 135 - 14	40300 LBS.
L.N.E.R. "10000" CLASS. 4-6-4 TYPE.	TONS. CWT. 166 - 0	32000 LBS.
L.M.S. "ROYAL SCOT" CLASS. 4-6-0 TYPE.	TONS. CWTS. 127 - 12	33150 LBS.
S.R. "LORD NELSON" CLASS. 4-6-0 TYPE.	TONS. CWTS. 140 - 4	33480 LBS.

British Rail

10. This ingenious poster was produced by the GWR to demonstrate that in the King class they had a more powerful locomotive than any of the other Groups in the late 1920s. Many would say that besides having the highest tractive effort and achieving tremendous performance, the Kings also won on sheer grace and balance of design. The resemblance between the Royal Scot and the Nelson can be accounted for by the plans of the latter being lent to Henry Fowler, the designer of the former. The larger Southern tender was needed because there were no water troughs on any part of that system and the extra height of the LNER tender was to accommodate the narrow corridor through which the relief crew could pass from train to footplate on the non-stop runs from London to Edinburgh.

not have begun to haul the loads, or show the fuel economy, of the post-1920 engines. Trains of 500 tons and over were frequent on the LNER and the sight of a Pacific with a pilot was almost unknown.

Liverpool Street, the other main terminus of the LNER had no new designs to show as yet, but the large Holden 4–6–0 locos, now repainted in LNER green, were impressive. At 8.30 every evening one of them gave a good demonstration of how a well-loaded train of about 400 tons, the 'Hook of Holland Boat Express', could be got away and up that stiff gradient to Bethnal Green,

without any great fuss. It was ever a favourite route with business travellers: a good dinner served on the way down to Harwich, a comfortable private cabin and berth on the steamer and an excellent breakfast to be had spinning across the Dutch fields the next morning. Under the new Group, however, it all improved steadily, including, in the 1930s, two of the largest and most luxurious cross-channel ships to date. For the rest, the LNER (Great Eastern section) had little more to show beside the fine old Claud Hamilton 4–4–0s still taking huge loads to Ipswich and Norwich, some still in their superb

11. LNER K3 2–6–0, Gresley's highly successful general utility loco which could take heavy goods trains at an average of 45 mph as well as running up to 75 mph with a passenger express. It was with this type that the designer tried out his famous 'conjugated valve gear' with the rocking shafts by which two sets of gear actuated the valves of all three cylinders. The same system was used on all the Pacifics as they developed ever greater performance and higher speeds.

blue livery lined out in red and yellow with a polished steel rim to the smokebox door. They had, too, the largest cabs of anything south of the Trent. Otherwise a big clutch of over 100 little 0–6–0 tank engines and a number of 2–4–2 tanks ran the entire London suburban service, the next busiest after Waterloo.

The other section of the LNER, the Great Central, was having a quiet time along at Marylebone, that neat, clean little terminus where it used to be said that it was 'an event' when a train came in. Built only in 1899 there was nothing very old there but the handsome Atlantic 4–4–2 class of 1904 and the larger Director class 4–4–0s of 1913 handled the

passenger expresses. Four-coupled and six-coupled tank engines dealt with the very comfortable London commuter service with its all-bogie trains, electric-lit and seemingly always clean. The line came into special prominence in 1924 and 1925 at the time of the British Empire Exhibition because, with great enterprise, it built a loop line right into a special station in the Exhibition grounds. On Saturday afternoons there seemed to be a non-stop service of trains coming off the GCR main line onto the loop, stopping at the station to set down and pick up, then puffing off round the sharp curve of the loop to rejoin the main line. There must have been quite a number of trains continually

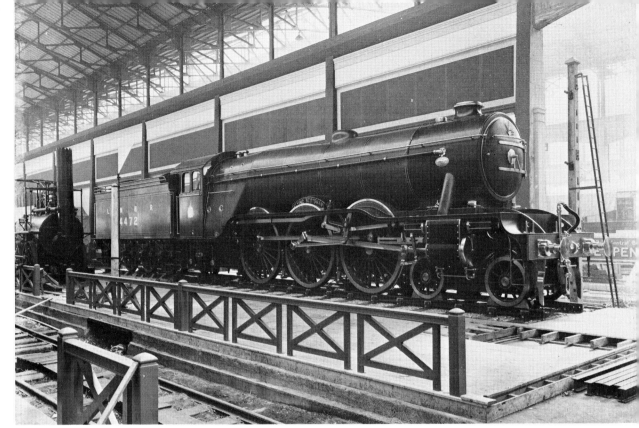

12. The LNER three-cylinder Pacific 4–6–2, 'Flying Scotsman', as shown in immaculate condition at the Wembley British Empire Exhibition in 1924. Adjoining it was the GWR Castle locomotive with her four cylinders. Both attracted admiring crowds of visitors who were allowed to climb up into the cabs of each. 'Locomotion' can be seen on the left-hand side of the picture.

'on the go' between Wembley and Marylebone. Also the great Exhibition was served by the Metropolitan from Baker Street and the main line from Euston through Wembley itself with a frequent service on the LMS (LNWR section) electrified line which also carried the through Watford trains from the Bakerloo tube line. Altogether that Exhibition depended considerably upon railways and its display of two famous newly built locomotives, the LNER Pacific 'Flying Scotsman' and the GWR 4–6–0 'Caerphilly Castle' led to an interesting rivalry which had long range effects.

Also facing the north and with lines starting steeply uphill was Euston, and that could be one of the most rewarding stations for variety in about 1924, though it was unlikely that one would see anything there that had been built since the 1914 war. The 4–4–0 engine, both the George V class and the Precursors, predominated but there were Claughtons and Experiments well in evidence among the 4–6–0s, the latter being like the Caledonian and the GER six-coupled engines with inside cylinders only. In the early 1920s it was still possible to see some of those heroic little 2–4–0s of the Precedent class which had been built by Webb as far back as 1874. They still handled some of the passenger work including continual duties as pilots. In 1924 one was to be seen piloting a Claughton

19

Ian Allan Collection

13. A superheated Precursor (ex-LNWR) 4–4–0 pounds up Camden Bank and through Chalk Farm on a heavy load of best LMS 'semi-fast' outer suburban stock. The rich lining-out and cleanliness of the carriages is typical of the 1920s.

4–6–0 on a huge Irish Mail of 14 coaches. To the disgust of many of the North Western drivers, soon after the Grouping the Midland Compound 4–4–0s began to appear on their lines, and then there was the building of a total 190 of them for use all over the LMS system. Good and economical as they were, especially in hilly conditions and with a moderate load, they were based upon a design dating back to 1902 (though modified in 1913), and could not compare with the new engines being produced for other railways at that time. Neither could they possibly haul – at least not without assistance – the trains of more than 400 tons which were common on the lines of the old LNWR. They had difficulty also in keeping time with the two-hour non-stop expresses from Euston to Birmingham: here

there was direct competition with the GWR which also did it in the same time. (The Compounds were, however, more successful and better liked in Scotland.)

Until the autumn of 1927 the one really big engine to be seen at Euston was the Claughton class four-cylinder and that dated from 1913. It was a fine locomotive but uncertain in its performance because it required above average skill to fire it successfully.

In the opening years of the LMS one of the major problems was the shortage of really powerful engines adequate for the services demanded on the West Coast route. Too many of the heavy trains out of Euston had to be double-headed and Sir Henry Fowler, now CME of the Group, whose Compound 4–4–0s

14. An LMS Royal Scot three-cylinder 4–6–0 pounding up Madeley Bank in 1928. The engine was then less than a year old and had yet to be fitted with the rather unsightly smoke deflectors which became standard for the class. The height of the boiler and shortness of the chimney made them inevitable. It is interesting to see that the second coach of the train appears to be a twelve-wheeler, either dining car or sleeper.

were good within limits on the Midland proceeded to design a large Compound Pacific loco. Memories of the gross inadequacies and troubles of the little Webb Compounds of the LNWR – around the turn of the century – were, however, still so vivid that powerful influences at Crewe refused to countenance the idea of further Compounds. Moreover experience with a borrowed GWR Castle suggested that a good 4–6–0 would do all that was required.

An augmented and accelerated summer service was to be run from Euston in 1927 and Fowler, lacking time to design a new engine and, in dire need, sent down to Waterloo where R. E. L. Maunsell had, in 1926, produced in the 'Lord Nelson' what was acclaimed as 'the most powerful engine' in Britain. In terms of tractive effort it beat the GWR 'Caerphilly Castle' by a small margin and the drawings of the Southern engine, generously loaned by Maunsell, provided an excellent basis for the famous Royal Scot 4–6–0 of which the remarkable number of 50 were ordered straight off from the North British Locomotive Company of Glasgow.

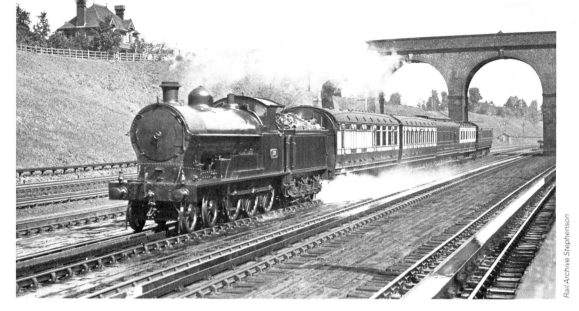

15. An up Birmingham two-hour express on the much photographed Bushey troughs, seemingly a bit over-powered by the LNWR 'Prince of Wales' 4–6–0 in 1925, since the train could not have weighed more than 150 tons. Two very fine, clean LNWR corridors precede a vintage Midland composite with its clerestory roof, then a pinched-up little LNWR corridor ending up with a modern one in LMS colours. No form of restaurant car is offered for the 112-mile journey.

16. In 1935 a very different train for the Birmingham run, drawn by a modern 4–6–0, a three-cylinder design derived from the pre-1914 Claughton class but with an enlarged boiler. Nicknamed the 'Baby Scots' they were thoroughly successful on all but the heaviest trains. This specimen is smartly turned out with whitened smokebox door-hinges and buffers. The passenger stock is modern throughout in LMS maroon and with elliptical roofs. The scene is Hatch End and the centre rail electrification to Watford is prominent on the right.

As everyone knows, the Scots were a great success but it was an indication of defects in the management at Crewe and Derby that they had to consult the Southern – which was not, some would say, the outstanding railway in steam development. It was without precedent to order 50 great engines straight off the drawing board and with no opportunity to try out a prototype in service first. However, with goodwill on the three sides – Maunsell, Fowler and most important of all the Glasgow firm of builders – all was well. Two years earlier they had built a number of the best King Arthurs for the Southern and it seemed that from the moment the Scots went into service the locomotive 'image' of the LMS began to improve. Not that there were no teething troubles. One remembers the way in which their exhaust steam failed to get away properly from their very short funnels, always there was a cloud of it seemingly clinging to the top of the boiler which seriously obstructed the driver's view at times. Later, they had those rather unsightly front-end side shields fitted, like many continental locos of the time (and indeed, as did the King Arthurs).

Not until the Royal Scots were delivered from the North British Locomotive Company of Glasgow, did the LMS possess a locomotive of modern design easily capable of hauling 400 tons, and more, non-stop single-handed from London to Carlisle. By then the LMS loco problems were on the way to solution and in 1930 a further step was taken in making reconstructions of the Claughtons with larger boilers and three (instead of four) cylinders. These became known as Baby Scots and at first sight they confused the observer by their remarkable resemblance to both the Claughtons and the Scots. However, they made a valuable addition to the locomotive strength of the Group being usable on both the LNWR and the Midland main lines.

In 1932 there came the bold move of the LMS management in appointing as Chief Mechanical Engineer W. A. Stanier, then Principal Assistant to the CME of the GWR at Swindon. This inaugurated the most successful period of locomotive design known to either Crewe or Derby and it had the effect of spreading the finer points of Great Western practice, as originated by the great G. J. Churchward, to each of the other three Groups. The free-steaming, tapered boiler, working at the higher pressure of 225 lb./ sq. in., and the particular cylinder and valve gear which used it most efficiently became part of all future LMS practice. So, in 1933 there came the famous Stanier Pacific the 'Princess Elizabeth' which, standing in the poky old Euston station, looked enormously impressive in its Midland style of livery which appeared to suit it to perfection. It seemed to be a perfect expression of its parentage which was in a sense 'LMS out of GWR'.

Then, a year later, came what many would regard as the most generally useful locomotive ever to run in Great Britain, the mixed traffic 4–6–0 known as the Stanier Black Five so-called because, as an economy measure in the 1930s, the LMS began to paint all its engines black (except the most favoured of the express passenger stock such as the Pacifics and Scots) and it was in Category 5 power classification. It was an extraordinarily adaptable engine, able, as O. S. Nock has written, 'to take heavy and fast express trains on virtually equal terms with the Royal Scots, do heavy goods work and run up to 90 mph on the moderately loaded express trains of the Midland line. They were used all over the LMS system from Wick to Bournemouth . . . ultimately there were 842 of the class in service.' Besides being reliable work-horses – though, alas, always black – they were in fact fine looking engines and were always popular with their drivers. The two cylinders were of the

17. One of the most successful and, in fact, most generally useful engines of the inter-war period, the LMS two-cylinder class 5 (known as the 'Black Five'), designed by W. A. Stanier after he came to Crewe from Swindon. A fine example of a mixed traffic engine, over 800 were built eventually and they worked literally 'from Bournemouth to Wick' and on every sort of train including some running up to 90 mph. Here is one bound for Carlisle and leaving Oxenholme on the fringe of the Lake District, with a characteristic tall LNWR signal in the background.

exceptionally large dimensions of $18\frac{1}{2} \times 28$ ins and coupled wheels of 6 ft diameter.

From the Pacific design mentioned earlier came the streamlined 'Coronation' of 1937 which made a record run Crewe to Euston at an average speed of 79·7 mph and helped considerably to publicise the advance in railway performance at a time when road competition was becoming more serious. This engine ran the famous Coronation Scot train competing with the LNER streamlined train to Edinburgh. It also led on, eventually, to further refinements culminating in the Pacific loco bearing the name of 'Sir William Stanier' built in 1947 which represented the final development of LMS steam, prior to nationalisation. So, after the

appointment of Stanier in 1932, the position was transformed; the earlier power shortage of the Group was completely remedied and the various types of engine available were fully equal to the tremendous demands made upon this huge system throughout the Second World War. To see how the Swindon influence spread to two other Groups we must now take a look at the GWR itself.

As we have seen, Collett's first post-war sensation was the 'Caerphilly Castle' of 1923 which was exhibited alongside Gresley's Pacific of 1922 at the Wembley exhibition in 1924. The public had the chance to clamber up wooden steps and stand on the actual footplate of each locomotive, and in this way they were much in

24

H. C. Casserley Collection

18. The historic 1925 locomotive exchange between LNER and GWR when for a week a Pacific engine of the former worked the 'Cornish Riviera' from Paddington to Plymouth, and the 4–6–0 'Pendennis Castle' worked a crack London to Leeds express. The immense interest in the affair is evident from the crowd of Press, officials and public gathered at the end of the departure platform at King's Cross as the Castle left on the first day.

the public eye. The Castles were known to be very speedy machines and the GWR publicised them heavily; they were somewhat smaller than the Gresley Pacifics and weighed less, yet they were said to be more powerful. Just how the idea of an interchange trial, or swap over of duties, came about is not known though it is believed to have emanated from Sir Felix Pole, then the General Manager of the GWR. When it was announced that for a week, in September 1925, a Castle was to take a crack Leeds express out one day and home to Kings Cross the next, while a Gresley Pacific was to handle the 'Cornish Riviera', the public interest was great. The Press entered into it all with zest and railway enthusiasts were fascinated to see front page pictures

of the GWR engine with Kings Cross station framing its exhaust steam, and the Pacific starting out from under the big girder bridge at Paddington.

Because the LNER only just kept time on the Plymouth runs and burnt more coal than the GWR locos, while the latter performed faster and more economically on the Leeds expresses, it was regarded as a 'victory' for the GWR. As Cecil J. Allen pointed out at the time, the Pacifics were under certain difficulties with their larger dimensions – greater height from the rail and greater length – in negotiating the sinuous parts of the GWR route, whereas the main line of the LNER was remarkably free from curves. The LNER engines did better towards the end of the

25

week as their drivers became more familiar with the gradients and speed restrictions of the Western line. To be set against the lower coal consumption of the Castles there was their greater initial cost of building and higher maintenance, due, in part, to the complications of their 225 lb./sq. in. of working pressure (against the 180 lb. of the Pacifics at that time). Their effect upon the track was also considered by some to be harder, their weight being concentrated upon ten wheels as opposed to twelve. It was said that some years of comparative trials would really be needed before the true cost 'per ton-mile' of the two locos could be assessed, but the LNER quickly recognised that the valve gear of the Castles was something from which they could learn. Gresley, as a direct result of this trial, redesigned the valve gear of his Pacifics and greatly improved their subsequent running. Thus, a most important element of Swindon practice spread to Doncaster, as well as to Crewe, and as will shortly be seen, it reached Ashford and Eastleigh also.

With very good reason GWR locomotives stood very high in public estimation in the 1920s. Quite apart from the much applauded performance of the 'Caldicote Castle' on the runs to Leeds, the average engine seen in Paddington station had an undoubted magnificence about it. Nowhere else could you hope to see so many locomotives with a brightly polished copper rim at the top of the funnel, their 'middle green' livery very smartly lined out in orange and black, their polished brass dome and safety valve casings as well as the beading on the edges of the splashers above the coupled wheels. Also, of course, with the LNWR, the GWR were one of the few lines which named all of its larger passenger engines, providing them with a handsome curved brass plate just above one of the splashers for the purpose.

In the early 1920s, wherever a Great Western engine came alongside that of another line (e.g. the Southern at Exeter) it always contrived to look bigger and more massive although the height of the boiler was no greater. Moreover, the blast of its exhaust seemed sharper and more powerful. I remember waiting for a connection to South Devon on the platform of St David's station and being amazed at the determined bark, a really explosive 'Chah! – Chah! – Chah!', emitted by a 4–4–0 just on a shunting operation. Whatever they did they seemed to do it with their might. Starting away as a passenger behind one of their two-cylinder engines – a 4–6–0 Saint or a 2–6–0 – one was distinctly aware of the thrust of the piston and the extra pull with each blast from the exhaust. It vanished as speed rose but it was a phenomenon I rarely experienced behind the engines of other railways (though it could happen behind the big American-built 2–8–2 engines to be found on the French railways just after the last war). It was only with two-cylinder engines that this was noticeable; with three- and four-cylinder locos the start was entirely smooth.

A young man of the period must be forgiven for recalling very vividly another feature peculiar to GWR engines, that was the hilariously rude noise which certain of their 0–6–0 saddle tanks seemed to enjoy emitting at intervals. It was all too easily imitated with the human mouth and probably had some bearing upon the use of the injector. Another interesting curiosity of those engines was the fitting of the coupling rods *outside* the frames; this practice was more common in Victorian times, especially on the Midland, but apart from its appearance on the GWR it was an unfamiliar sight to most southerners.

While the running of its steam services often seemed disappointing in the years after the last war, there can be no doubt about the splendid performances put up by GWR Saints, Stars,

C. R. L. Coles

19. GWR 'Morning Star', the famous Churchward four-cylinder 4–6–0, approaching Paddington about 1934. From this engine Churchward's successor, Collett, derived the larger and still more powerful Castle and King classes. The Star tenders always look strangely small for an engine which regularly hauled the 'Cornish Riviera' on its 226-mile non-stop run, but that is testimony to its efficient and economical design and to the good provision of water troughs on the line.

20. 'Carmarthen Castle' about to depart from Paddington in 1930. Its Star parentage is obvious but differences are the side-window of the roomier cab (with its tip-up seats) and the prominent steam pipes from the smoke-box down to the cylinders; the heads of the inside cylinders are plainly visible above the buffer-beam. Many would say that it was the best proportioned and most handsome locomotive design the world has ever seen, as well as – in the words of O. S. Nock – the most famous and successful.

Rail Archive Stephenson

21. Maunsell's Lord Nelson class four-cylinder 4–6–0, no. 856, 'Lord St Vincent', on an up Dover Continental Express passing Folkestone Junction, the point from which the Folkestone Harbour branch drops steeply down to sea level. The engine is newly built and has not yet had the steam deflectors fitted. Flat-cars next to the engine are loaded with the containers for registered luggage which have been swung direct from ship to train. Next come three of the curious straight-sided corridors, with end access only, which the SECR built for their boat trains and further down there is a Pullman car. Altogether it is a good load for a steeply graded line, even for a Nelson which for a short time had the highest tractive effort of any locomotive in Britain.

Castles and Kings in the 1920s and 1930s. One of the lines which showed them at their most brilliant was the Paddington to Birmingham (Snow Hill) run. Though it has some quite stiff climbs there are equivalent descents. Never did speed seem to drop below about 50 mph uphill and on the down gradients there were regular bursts of 80 mph and over – in 1925 it was said to offer higher maximum speeds in regular service than any other line. It all seemed to be designed to show off the capability of Churchward and Collett design and the vigour and enterprise of Western enginemen. The pleasure to the traveller was enhanced by the beauty of the country, including part of the Chilterns,

through which he passed. It was in advertising this particular route that the GWR produced one of its very striking posters – at least by the standards of the times. Showing the bold heading 'London – Birmingham Two Hour Express', it depicted a head-on view of the handsome Castle locomotive at the Paddington buffer-stops, a relaxed and happy looking driver and fireman leaning out of the cab while a prosperous looking, red-faced gent smartly dressed and in spats put up his hand to grasp the driver's saying, 'A fine run, thank you!'

With equally good work achieved on the South Wales and West of England routes it was not surprising that Swindon methods of steam

22. SR three-cylinder Schools class no. 927, 'Clifton'. Each engine bore the name of a famous public school and the class, by Maunsell, was said to be the most powerful 4–4–0 in Europe. Originally designed in 1930 for the Hastings line with its steep gradients, awkward curves and tight tunnel clearances, the 'Schools' later proved outstandingly successful in the last years of steam, working on the Portsmouth and Bournemouth lines. Here no. 927 is seen passing through Petersfield on a Portsmouth express in 1937. Conductor rails are already laid beside the track.

design were closely followed and Eastleigh and Ashford took note.

Although much capital cost and effort were being devoted to electrification on the Southern, steam was not neglected. It had still more than ten years to run even on the Brighton line and up to fourteen years on the Portsmouth, while it would be well into the 1960s before the smoke would disappear from the Bournemouth and Exeter lines. For the steam enthusiast there was much to be seen in the years immediately after the Grouping.

Robert Urie, successor to Dugald Drummond, had designed in 1914 an excellent 4–6–0 mixed traffic engine with two large outside cylinders which performed very heavy duties right through the war and without any general repair. By 1918 he had produced similar engines all superheated but with slightly larger 6 ft 7 in. coupled wheels. He retired with the absorption of the LSWR into the Southern Group but he had given the line the basis of a very fine and extremely useful locomotive.

Urie's successor was Richard Maunsell from the former SE & CR at Ashford. To youthful South Western enthusiasts it appeared monstrous that a railway with such a chequered past could have anything to teach us at Waterloo or Eastleigh. What we did not at first realise was that Maunsell had had experience at Swindon imbibing the virtues of long valve travel, higher steam pressures and better front-end design, and that he had already produced for the SECR a large 4–4–0 which handled heavy boat trains

C. R. L.

23. Drummond T9 (ex-LSWR) no. 114 as re-built by Maunsell for the Southern in 1927. The superheater, extended smoke-box – to say nothing of the long stove-pipe chimney – gave these fine little engines another twenty-five to thirty years of life so that some ran for about sixty years in all. Deservedly called the 'Greyhounds', if not grossly over-loaded they could run at well over 80 mph. Their exceptionally large grate area, due to a long wheelbase, enabled them to raise steam very rapidly. Here we see no. 114 at Winchester City on a cross-country train, with part GWR stock, bound for Southampton.

very well and a quite excellent 2–6–0 mixed traffic engine which looked remarkably like a GWR one. It had a tapered boiler, 200 lb. pressure and Ross-Poppet safety valves which blew off with a most impressive roar (its successors were soon to be seen in many parts of the Southern system tackling almost every sort of job). Now, here is where the special value of Swindon ideas and their influence upon the third Group can be seen. Maunsell, who had served his apprenticeship at Inchicore with the Great Southern & Western of Ireland and had also worked for the Lancashire & Yorkshire at Horwich, was happy to take on another

Swindon man, H. Holcroft, when he applied for a job at Ashford. Together they accomplished a great deal in the early years of loco design on the Southern and much of it was Swindon inspired.

The first major achievement was the creation of a new fleet of 4–6–0s which became the King Arthur class, each bearing a name associated with the Arthurian legend. A pleasing feature of them to LSWR enthusiasts was that superficially they looked like an advanced – and more powerful – edition of the Drummond 4–6–0s of pre-war days but, while based upon Robert Urie's express locos of the 736 class they embodied a higher boiler pressure and a much improved front-end. As Hamilton Ellis remarked in his *Four Main Lines*, they were 'one of the most useful and reliable express passenger engines the country had yet known'. Some were built at Eastleigh inheriting certain parts from earlier Drummond 4–6–0s which Urie had planned to rebuild, and twenty were produced by the North British Locomotive Company of Glasgow. These latter were the more handsome, with huge polished steel hinges to the smokebox doors like those of the Midland and the Great Northern engines. Their Walschaert's valve gear with its vigorous 'elbow' motion seemed more graceful than some and it emitted an interesting spitting sound with each thrust of the pistons so that it came out like a swift 'tick – tick – tick' as the engine ran past at speed.

The King Arthurs, as evolved by Maunsell and Holcroft, must really be seen as one of the 'greats' of their day. Besides their wonderfully free running which enabled them often to clock up their 90 mph on the Salisbury to Exeter switchback – 76 miles in 78 minutes with 14 'on' over steep gradients was another feat – they could also punch their way along keeping time with a fully laden Bournemouth express to which an extra three or four corridor coaches had been added to convey passengers for some smallish liner at Southampton, or maybe the comparatively few who were joining a German or French ship calling in there. These same engines fitted with six-wheel tenders also did good work on the Central section, the former LBSCR, until electrification in 1933 and, of course, upon the Eastern (SECR) section with the heavy boat trains to Folkestone and Dover.

As the traffic to the Continent grew under the Southern's vigorous promotion, larger engines were in demand capable of hauling trains of 500 tons over the steeply graded routes to the Kent coast. These were produced in the shape of the Lord Nelson class with their four cylinders and with cranks set at 135 degrees to produce the curious 'eight-impulse' drive to each revolution of the wheels. With their 220 lb. per square inch boiler pressure and tractive effort of 33,500 lb. they were, on paper, the most powerful engines in the country for about a year. Their very soft exhaust with double the normal number of 'puffs' was strangely misleading for they performed well – if not so outstandingly, for their size, as did the Arthurs.

The third major achievement of Mr Maunsell was his 4–4–0 Schools class. Described by railwaymen as a 'three-quarter Nelson' it had three cylinders against the four of the larger engine but in most other respects it followed the same pattern, though the boiler was actually a shortened version of the King Arthurs. The Schools were light on coal yet could handle up to 450 tons and keep time. Intended primarily for the awkward Hastings line with its reduced clearances and steep gradients, the class distinguished itself over much of the Southern, save on the West of England line which was well catered for by Nelsons and Arthurs. In the opinion of O. S. Nock 'they were without any doubt the most successful 4–4–0 locomotive ever to run in Great Britain' – considerable praise for the Group which at that time was putting so much of its development capital and general resources into electrification.

The other remarkable success of the Maunsell era was the rebuilding of the Drummond 4–4–0 locomotives. While still doing good work, most of them were between twenty-five and thirty years old and though Urie had rebuilt the 4–6–0s and the largest 4–4–0s there were still a large number of the Greyhounds working with saturated steam and their essentially Victorian looking, flat-chested, smokeboxes. Southern policy dictated that all of them, the T9 class, should be rebuilt with extended smokebox and it must have been one of the best value-for-

24. The unique ten-coupled (0–10–0) four-cylinder engine designed by the Midland Railway solely for banking trains up the Lickey Bank between Bromsgrove and Blackwell on the main line from Bristol to Birmingham. It is a busy stretch of line – two miles at the tremendous gradient of 1 in 37 – and this engine was able to do the work of two 0–6–0 goods engines, spending all its working life running up and down that one section. Starting away from the lower station is an interesting assortment of stock: Midland clerestory coaches, a narrow LNWR with low roof and beyond it probably GWR. The sharp upward curve of the gradient is clearly visible beyond the station platform.

money operations of its kind ever undertaken. For less than £500 spent a T9 showed a saving of 4·7 lb. of coal per mile and its performance improved out of all knowledge. It seemed that one never had a poor run behind a superheated Drummond 4–4–0, whether a T9 or a larger L12. They had a different 'feel' about them altogether. If you were leaving from a terminus you were immediately aware of a different sound from the engine even as it came on to the train to couple up. When it started the extra power developed from the superheating of the

steam, almost comparable to a supercharger in a racing car, enabled the rebuilt T9 with its sharper sounding exhaust to accelerate faster. The treatment was a wonderful new lease of life for the engines and I recall a most sprightly run behind a 35-year-old one on a short Southampton boat train in 1933 – curiously enough it was all (pre-Southern) LSWR corridor stock – and my last run, in 1950, was with a 50-year-old T9 when we had a quite exciting journey down the line to Bude from Halwill Junction in North Cornwall. The proud old driver in charge

32

remarked to me, as a Bulleid Pacific danced away from us at Halwill, its coupled wheels slipping and not gripping too well, 'And if that engine lasts *half* the time this one has done, we can be very thankful!'

Such rebuilds were an important part of the railway scene in the 1920s and the LNER successfully treated many of the 4–4–0s and the 4–6–0s of the former GER in this way. Fitted with superheater and extended smokebox they continued to give good service over many years. The little North Staffordshire was also active with their 4–4–0s and of course the Midland had engaged extensively in the practice earlier.

One other important branch of loco production should also be mentioned – the freight engine. Though built a little before our period, the Midland four-cylinder 0–10–0 should be recalled as a unique engine which dealt with trains of all kinds; the so-called 'Big Bertha' was built especially for the 2½-mile Lickey Bank of 1 in 37½ on the Bristol to Birmingham line. Her life was confined to bouts of about eight minutes of blasting her way up, mainly at the rear of goods trains, between the stations of Bromsgrove and Blackwell on a section of dead straight track. When the train reached the upper station the 'Banker' came off, crossed over and as soon as convenient ran back down the gradient. It was wonderful to watch the operation from the top station whence the rails curved over from the level stretch in the platform and dived downwards. A train climbing up seemed to have two pillars of fire above it at night and of white cloud by day. This great 0–10–0 spent her whole career of thirty years doing the work otherwise often needing two

0–6–0s at the rear and always the train engine at the head of the train.

The LMS, beside their fleet of 580 modern 0–6–0s (derived from a Fowler design, two-cylinder and superheated) which handled the vast bulk of the freight traffic, also had some interesting Beyer-Garratt 2–6–0 + 0–6–2s. In effect, these were 'twin' locomotives with the two sets of coupled wheels sharing a huge boiler between them; they were able to be manned by one crew. A later design was Stanier's great four-cylinder 2–8–0 of which numbers were also built for service overseas during the 1939 war, and Gresley also built a three-cylinder engine of the same 2–8–0 type for use on the LNER. The GWR had earlier had 2–8–0 freight engines in addition to its great number of 0–6–0s, which on every Group carried the lion's share of the nation's goods at a time when there were no up-to-date dual carriageway roads and the six or eight wheel lorry was virtually unknown.

Before leaving the ever fascinating subject of the steam locomotive in our period, the once popular 2–4–0s should not be overlooked. They performed a great deal of express passenger work in the late 1870s and 1880s and were specially prominent on the Midland, LNWR, GER and the NER. Though relegated to local trains by the 1920s, they were doing useful work and certainly the famous LSWR Adams 0–4–2 Jubilees of 1887 (which may be regarded as very similar) were regularly active as late as 1936. Towards the end of their days they were especially associated with the working of troop trains, race specials and excursion trains, also on some lines the 2–4–0s acted as pilots when there was double-heading to be done.

3
Carriages

The first 20 years of the century had shown an enormous advance in the design of rolling stock, but at the time of the Grouping in 1923 there was still great variety. Three or four types of coach might be found in the make-up of one train, as well as the chance of finding some carriages in the colours of the original pre-grouped lines while others might sport the new Group colours. Many an early LMS express presented an extraordinarily untidy roof line in the assortment of its stock. Behind the tender of a Claughton 4–6–0 there might be a little old LNWR corridor coach looking short and narrow but strongly built in timber, then perhaps a handsome Midland vehicle with its beautiful clerestory roof, followed by medium-sized LNWR corridors with eliptical roofs flanking the completely Edwardian-looking restaurant car (again with a clerestory roof and splendid six-wheel bogies). Thus there were four distinct levels of roof and there might be three different colours: the fine old plum and spilt milk of the LNWR, the genuine Derby crimson lake of the independent Midland and its rather poor imitation, the maroon colour adopted by the LMS. On occasion there could also be the chocolate colour of the Lancashire & Yorkshire and the blue of the Furness Railway.

The GWR, though it had remained entirely 'itself' in the Grouping and had suffered no great upheaval, could yet show a similar miscellany of

stock on an important train. A train would be 'strengthened' by adding an old early 1900s corridor with its heavy looking clerestory roof, then would follow the more modern stock, roomier and with eliptical roofs, but then the effect would be spoilt by some of the vehicles being painted in the earlier chocolate and cream while others would be in the later crimson lake style.

The South Western was in a rather similar position having decided in 1921 to introduce green for their steam-hauled carriages in place of the 'salmon' for upper panels and dark brown below the waist. This was attractive when newly painted but weathered badly and, long before the automatic carriage washing sheds were available, was apt to look decidedly shabby. Then, as the newer all-metal covered Bournemouth expresses appeared painted green all over, this was adopted as the livery for all stock. It had, of course, been the style for all electric trains since they were first introduced in 1915. So, here was a typical LSWR train, sometimes with an odd little low-roofed coach dating from the 1880s (they had bogies and travelled quite well) in the salmon livery, then a carriage of somewhat higher roof-line as built in the early 1900s. After these might come a lavatory set in the new green and possibly some of the new all-metal coaches looking bigger in every way than the others. It all added much to the variety and

Rail Archive Stephenson

25. This LMS (Midland) St Pancras to Manchester express near Mill Hill in 1926 presents several curious features. It is essentially a Midland train headed by a classic Deeley Compound, 4–4–0 three-cylinder, with tender fitted for oil firing in view of the coal strike that year. The leading coach is isolated from the rest of the train by the little LNWR brake van; then come a genuine Midland clerestory brake composite followed by a modern Reid coach with elliptical roof. The dining car and the rest of the train could be the normal Midland stock.

interest of railways though already there were the beginnings of uniformity and a tendency for all new stock built after the war to utilise the full loading gauge, building the body out to a width of nine feet instead of the former 8 ft 6 in. This was a great advantage in the corridor carriage and made the seating of four-a-side tolerable in third class – though to those who had grown accustomed to the much wider foot-boards of the narrower stock, the foot-boards of the new stock seemed very poor things. They were so narrow by comparison with those of the older coaches that the seasoned daily traveller, all too likely to board his train 'in motion' if in a hurry,

found that he had to watch his step far more carefully.

This leads on to a digression but one of historic importance. In the days of steam the start of a train was more leisurely because the power of acceleration was much less than that of the later diesel or electric train. Catching your train from a London terminus from which you were a 'regular' you almost certainly had your methods of sneaking on to the platform at the last possible moment even if the barrier were officially closed. In steam days there would be an engine (standing uncoupled) which had brought the train in to the platform and, usually, this

35

26. Gladstone class 0–4–2 of the former LBSCR, built in 1891, here repainted in Southern livery with the word just discernible on her tender. The first four coaches are LSWR non-lavatory third class, the rest are low-roofed 'Brighton' stock, not luxurious but noted for their smooth running. The scene is Copyhold Junction near Haywards Heath.

engine would also start the train on its journey. If, as you ran past it, the guard's whistle having already blown, you heard a 'pluck' from the engine as the regulator was opened there was still time to make a dash for the roomy foot-board of the rear coach and scramble in safely. If, on the other hand you heard the 'klonk' of the engine buffers engaging those of the rear coach and the first heavy blasts from the funnel it was probably wiser to consider from which platform the next train to your destination would depart. At all events the introduction of the wider stock with its narrower foot-boards discouraged the practice and electric trains virtually put an end to it – their acceleration was too sharp – and on all

but the oldest stock (made out of old steam carriages) I would risk nothing more than a swift hop if the train had *just* begun to move.

By the time of the Grouping one could be reasonably confident that any long distance train would consist of corridor carriages so that there need be no anxiety over calls of nature en route. At holiday time, however, there was a tendency for some lines to drag out of a siding rather ancient coaches in order to 'strengthen' a popular train. Passengers would be thankful to take a seat in it, in preference to standing in the corridor, and in the heat of the moment might not realise that such a vehicle had neither corridor nor lavatory compartment. In early

27. An early King Arthur class two-cylinder 4–6–0, no. 450, 'Sir Kay', of the Southern approaches Clapham Junction with a West of England express in 1925. She will certainly exceed 80 mph once or twice before Salisbury (and more times if the same engine works through to Exeter). The train has been 'strengthened' in the spartan manner of those days by the addition of three old non-corridor coaches at the front, the third a gas-lit veteran of the 1880s. The rest are pre-1914 corridors with the clerestory marking the dining 'saloon' which will almost certainly come off at Exeter.

Southern days I once saw a Saturday afternoon express arriving at the old Queen Street station at Exeter after its 88-mile run from Salisbury with a couple of such coaches right at the end which did not reach the platform. An elderly gentleman leaning out of the window of one of them, plainly in need, had some hard words for the platform staff, demanding to be let out. His cruel predicament was resolved by the provision of a short ladder. The train would have been divided there and after the Plymouth portion in front had gone on its way the rear coaches would doubtless have been drawn into the platform,

but it was an awkward business until, after a few years the station was rebuilt and the platforms lengthened.

The presence of an old coach between the engine and the rest of a train of modern carriages must have caused anxiety to some observant passengers. A wooden veteran could run well and sometimes more quietly than its modern counterpart but its creaking bodywork and springy joints made one wonder what might happen to it, between 120 tons of steel in front and 400 tons of train behind, in the event of a serious mishap.

37

28. The GWR in full glory, recovered from the 1914 war and not yet nationalised. The up 'Torbay Express', after its *Rail Archiv* whirlwind descent from Whitehall summit, slows on the sweeping curve into Taunton station. The coaches are fairly gleaming in their chocolate and cream livery while the King displays all the traditional GWR characteristics to perfection: the copper-capped chimney shortened from the Castle style on account of the larger boiler, the big brass safety valve, the inside cylinder heads showing below the smokebox and that large tender proudly displaying the words 'Great Western' – no mere initials for them!

Prior to the 1914 war many lines had begun building the wider and higher carriages but still with much outside panelling and made of wood throughout apart from the under-carriage. They blossomed, especially upon the East Coast and West Coast routes to Scotland though the Midland was only beginning to forsake its clerestory roof in the carriages built towards the end of its independence by R. W. Reid. The GWR was generous in its carriage dimensions for main line stock and both the LBSCR and the LSWR had produced a few coaches of similar size by 1914 but were prevented from continuing them by the war. The bodywork was still wood throughout with the usual elaborate exterior panelling.

The LSWR was the first line to break with tradition by having carriages with steel panels instead of wood on their exterior. Naturally, this eliminated the panels which for so long had been a feature of all railway carriage building, though there was still a tendency for the 'lining-out' in the livery to follow what would have been the pattern of the panels had they been of timber. The coaches in question were the so-called 'Tea Sets' built for the Bournemouth

29. The British Empire Exhibition of 1925 (its second year). One of the constant stream of LNER Specials from Marylebone to the Exhibition slowing down to take the branch line into the Grounds. There it described a loop and after the one stop, to set down and pick up, it returned to the main line of the former GCR. The carriage stock is typical of the very high standard of suburban travel on that line.

service for which there had been very few corridor trains. They were just the thing for the journey of only 108 miles. The space of one compartment in a side-corridor coach was fitted out as a pantry which served very satisfactory trays of tea, egg dishes and grills to those in the 'Tea Set'. As a youthful season ticket holder (we did not know the word 'commuter' in the 1920s) I sometimes took a joy ride to Waterloo in an early evening train of such coaches from Bournemouth which stopped at my home station of Surbiton. They seemed beautiful vehicles: the third class upholstered in the rich brown plush formerly used for the second class

(abolished in 1918) and with three lights in the roof instead of the one cluster as before. They had all the nice little features which we still associated with the best South Western coaches like touches of gilding here and there, arms for the corner seats and a discreet patterned decoration on the roof – altogether they *looked* like second class. And in the first class there was very handsome rep upholstery, the same as in the dining cars, nicely curved backs to the corner seats and neatly disappearing folding arms for the three-a-side seating and of course carpets on the floor for the firsts and linoleum for the thirds. Also, there was the curious LSWR pro-

30. Though the engine is in LNER livery this photo can be said to depict the Great Central line at its finest: the handsome 4–6–0 by J. G. Robinson heading the neat train of uniform elliptical roofed corridor coaches with restaurant car. Running through the lovely country of the Chilterns and then the 'hunting shires', this train offered some of the most comfortable accommodation ever created for third-class passengers.

vision for narrow tables to be set up in the compartments.

By degrees this type of coach became a standard for the whole of the Southern and by 1926, under Maunsell's direction, they were to be found on the best of the West of England trains. Furthermore, an excellent advance from the safety point of view, was that they were close-coupled and fitted with the Buckeye automatic coupling. This had been used for Pullman cars and on all the corridor coaches of the East Coast route for many years. It provided a much wider and shorter vestibule connection between coaches which was easier for passengers to negotiate and was much less likely to break apart

in the event of a derailment (though, strangely, it was not taken up by the other two Groups, the LMS and GWR).

In the opinion of those familiar with these latter day Southern coaches, including Mr Hamilton Ellis, they offered the most comfortable third class seats in the country; being a little deeper, supporting more of one's thighs and they were beautifully sprung. New LMS carriages were very fine to look at and soft to sit in but their seats lacked depth, you seemed to sit on the edge of them (and how a generously built man like Josiah Stamp ever 'passed' them one could not imagine). Then the LNER from 1933 went in for a lot of open thirds with an individual

31. Metropolitan out in the country. From Baker Street to Harrow-on-the-Hill all was electric haulage but thereafter this unique 4–4–4 steam tank engine, designed by Charles Jones, took over. Here it is seen climbing towards Chesham in the Chilterns where, north of Rickmansworth, the line has a gradient of 1 in 100 for many miles. In that residential section trains stopped at every station, which meant hard work for both fireman and locomotive.

back to each seat but these were so concave that any man of even moderate height – let alone a six-footer – had to sit round-shouldered and hunched up, or stuff a coat into the void behind him.

This period of the mid-twenties saw the break in the near 30-year-old tradition of the side-corridor coach though the GWR, in the main, remained faithful to it. Derby brought out a handsome Midland style of centre-corridor vehicle with tables for four each side of the gang-way. They were also handy to use as restaurant cars when the pressure for meals en route grew to necessitate the use of the separate kitchen car which became usual on the most important of the LMS expresses. They were an excellent innovation. Built of steel throughout and fire-proof to a high standard, they had a side corridor down which one's feet crunched on a metallic floor and with the separate dining cars fore and aft it was said that they could serve 150 people at a sitting. The London–Manchester run, for example, on weekdays must have had an exceptionally high proportion of expense account men breakfasting or dining on the train and there can be no doubt that the LMS knew what they were about in making such ample provision.

One can see the railways' case for preferring, in the main, the open saloon type of coach, but for many travellers they are anathema. There is

Lens of

32. The original 'South Western Electric' dating from 1915, which became the basis of the Southern Electric from 1923. Built up from the six and eight-wheel stock of the early 1900s, the carriages ran at first in sets of three coaches with a pointed 'wind-cutter' end at front and rear. Rough riding and boney in their original form, they had good acceleration and were later worked in sets of four coaches with much improved upholstery and springing. The compartment style of carriage ensured rapid loading and unloading on suburban work, even if it did make the trains difficult to heat.

no sort of privacy: the penetrating voice, the crying child or the roars of tipsy laughter are audible to the entire coach-load and on a long journey the continual traffic of passengers which used to go along the corridor, to and from lavatory or restaurant car, now brushes one's elbow. Ideally, for many of us there should be both types of seating available on long distance trains, as was indeed the custom with many of the carriages of the old Southern Railway.

A great advantage of the open saloon type of carriage was that it tended generally to be warmer because the door to the outside was usually at the end in a separate vestibule (the one danger was the fresh-air fiend who, in cold weather, seldom realised the draught he inflicted upon those seated far behind him). On the other hand, for a 'sitting up' night journey the separate compartment won every time, especially if you had the luck to travel only two-a-side. To be able to stretch at least one's legs on the seat was almost as good as the third class sleeper when it came in 1928.

Among other carriage developments at this time was the emergence of new Pullman cars for the Southern's continental boat trains from Victoria to Dover and Folkestone. All were named, in accordance with Pullman custom in those days and it is tempting to think of Sir Herbert Walker and his fellow directors – in all probability – sitting down solemnly to approve the names of 'Aurelia', 'Marjorie', 'Medusa', 'Sappho' and 'Viking'. The old SECR railway had never built any restaurant cars of its own, depending instead upon Pullmans, but the latter, including the service to the ordinary compartments of their smartly uniformed stewards, must have saved the life of many a returning English man and woman with a good pot of freshly made tea or real coffee and freshly cut sandwiches after the discomforts of a Channel crossing 50 years ago. The LNER also made use of Pullmans on the 'Queen of Scots' and the 'Master Cutler', as did the GWR briefly on the 'Torbay Limited'.

It was noticeable how the poorer relations among the once independent railways began to benefit from the 'cast-offs' of the richer lines. To be specific, the Great North of Scotland ran restaurant cars which had been superannuated by the LNER from its services further south. The Great Eastern's Clacton express served an excellent breakfast from a spacious old Great Northern car whose former customers – perhaps on a Leeds express – were then enjoying a meal in one of Mr Gresley's latest three-coach articulated sets with kitchen in the middle and all cooking done electrically. Or again, the Southern transferred some of its oldest corridor coaches – solidly made and smooth running but rather mean in their dimensions – to the LBSCR and the SECR while the West of England and Bournemouth travellers enjoyed the more spacious stock newly built by Mr Maunsell.

Oddly enough, the South Eastern's rather florid – if handsome – red and black upholstery seemed to dominate all new carriages for some years (rather than the sober brown plush of the old LSWR second class or what Mr Ellis termed 'the grim uncut moquette of geometrical red on black' of the old thirds). The SECR cloth had looked terrible when old and shabby in ill-cared for carriages but fresh and properly brushed down it was rather good. Hesitantly, we agreed that it was 'not bad'. When it appeared in some new electric trains in 1925, on the Guildford via Cobham line it looked excellent and was in fact far superior to the upholstery formerly used on the Southern Electrics.

There is no doubt that each of the four Groups in its own way tried hard during the decade of the 1920s to make good the sadly run down condition of their lines after the four years of hard wartime use and minimum maintenance. The traveller in 1920 who went abroad for ten years returning in 1930 would have observed very great changes and improvements; had he waited another five years to the famous Jubilee year of King George V he would have seen the railways of Britain at what many would regard as their high water mark for efficiency, service to the traveller and, it must be admitted, sheer interest of operation to the railway buff.

Like the Southern, the LMS was able to advertise a very impressive programme of carriage building in addition to its massive attack on the engine problem. An outlay was made of over £14 million, much of it on its express passenger stock, corridor coaches, sleeping cars and the steel kitchen cars (a feature of the latter's equipment being the Australian hardwood which made them virtually non-flammable). During the 1920s and in view of this provision of new corridor coaches, there was a steady policy

33. The LNER down 'Silver Jubilee' near Ganwick on its run from King's Cross to Newcastle-on-Tyne which was accomplished in four hours at an average speed of over 70 mph. Introduced in 1936, the high-speed train was named in honour of the twenty-fifth year of the reign of King George V. It was the pioneer streamlined express in this country, attracting enormous interest and highly favourable publicity with the Gresley 'A4' Pacific and the specially designed coaches all painted in silver. The original train as seen here consisted of only seven coaches and the principles of articulation used reduced the number of bogies and thus the weight of the train, as well as adding to the smoothness of running at high speeds.

of scrapping the older gas-lit stock. This meant that many of the handsome clerestory Midland carriages disappeared – inevitably, because some of them were as much as 25 years old. Three of them were part of the make-up of a night mail train from Leeds to Bristol which in 1928 crashed into the engine of a goods train which was shunting its trucks into a siding at Charfield. Wreckage piled up against an over-bridge at that point. A cloud of gas from broken storage cylinders below the old gas-lit coaches was immediately ignited and the first six vehicles of the Mail were burnt out resulting in the death of sixteen passengers. Fifteen and eighteen years earlier comfortable but gas-lit MR coaches had come in for criticism after the ghastly fires they had caused in accidents at Ais Gill and Hawes Junction (on the Settle and Carlisle line); it was tragic that some of the comparatively few of such carriages still in service should have claimed their toll yet again. The new stock was particularly welcome. It then

34. This photo shows the neatness of the connection between the coaches of the 'Silver Jubilee', the elimination of suction between them, the articulated bogie and the special skirting to reduce wind resistance below the coaches.

became an interesting custom for that line, the LMS, to use different forms of 'Empire' hardwoods for its carriage furnishing and a neat little label in each compartment informed one whether it was Nigerian Teak or Australian Karri or whatever. All this new stock was, of course, built up to the limits of the loading gauge and with their eliptical roofs (in place of the old clerestory) the LMS trains began to lose their former somewhat ragged 'up and down' – if interesting – appearance, replaced with coaches of uniform height.

At the same time a very great improvement on London Tube trains made its first appearance: that of automatic doors. Until then passengers'

entry was by open gangways at the ends of cars controlled by folding gates. One gateman stood on the gangway between each of two cars and he opened and shut the gates at each station. Access to the interior of the cars (from the gangways) was by sliding doors which he also had to work. When all were aboard and the gates closed each conductor rang a mechanical bell which sounded in the next gangway beyond him until on the leading car it sounded in the motorman's compartment. At every station there was a considerable racket as first the steel gates clashed to one after another, then the bells sounded in sequence and finally the train moved off. In rush hours passengers used to travel standing on

45

35. Perhaps the acme of first-class luxury in a corridor compartment of the 'Silver Jubilee' train of the LNER. The 'jazz' type of upholstery is typical of the age and was to be found also in many of the new long-distance electric trains of the Southern. The square cushions of artificial silk in the corners are an unusual feature, indicating a great desire to please. The smallish window seems a mistake, reducing the view compared to what one used to see through the 'drop light' of the door plus the two side windows. However, to have only end doors to the coach reduced the risk of draughts and saved heating.

those open gangways – I used to enjoy thudding along under the Thames on the short-length rails of the Bakerloo in the strange warm air – but it led to awkward mix-ups at the stops when passengers had somehow to compress themselves and reduce the space they occupied in order to allow the gate to open inwards. That one could only get in or out from the ends of the cars was a terrible nuisance and made passengers reluctant to retreat into the middle. The continual cry 'Pass further down the car!' was uninviting when it might mean your being jammed in there when you came to your stop. Thus two sets of sliding automatic doors in the middle giving direct access to the cars were an immense advantage and immediately eliminated the need for about four gatemen per train. Instead there was just one guard in the rear car

who closed all the doors by pressing one button and then gave the starting signal to his motor-man by pressing another. It was just one of many refinements which the 1920s put on a late Victorian invention, the deep level tube railway.

While on the subject of the London tube rolling stock one must mention the variety of carriages which developed on other electric services, namely those of the LMS and the Southern. The former ran from Euston to Watford Junction, along the old main line of the LNWR, and the former North London Railway from Broad Street to Richmond. Originally finished in the livery of the LNWR (later painted in LMS colours), the carriages were furnished in the sober red and black upholstery of that line – so that you thought you might almost be starting off to the Lake District or

Scotland, and best of all the running of the carriages was so good that it felt like it. Even the local lines from Euston (whence there were six tracks) were laid with 60 ft rails, so that 50 years ago one had the '1–2, 3–4' rhythm then peculiar to the Premier line and the design of the bogies was such that one seemed to glide along in a manner totally different from that of travelling on the Southern Electric or the District. True, these (now) LMS electrics had not the acceleration of the Southern but they demonstrated that suburban electric trains *could* be as smooth as steam.

To be fair to the Southern it must be remembered that their electrification was begun early in the 1914 war and it had to be undertaken economically. Many four- and six-wheel carriages, some of them already 20 years old or more, were refurbished and put upon new under-carriages to live again as bogie stock. The carriages were a little on the short side, much of the track of the local lines was still 30 ft and there was much clatter of wheels but the acceleration was good. In the early trains there was a most disconcerting tendency for the lights to dim when the power was first applied, to such an extent that one could barely read. As speed rose the light improved and when the motorman switched off power in order to coast into the station, perhaps half a mile away, the light then became brilliant.

These vagaries were overcome in the new stock built about 1925. It followed the new style of Southern carriage building with an all-metal exterior, deeply sprung seating in both classes with the aforesaid SECR style of red and black in the third class and the distinctly luxurious 'Saladin Rep Moquette' for the first. At one jump the recently despised SR was able to offer some of the most comfortable suburban trains in the whole country. The quality of the actual ride – the smoothness over the track – was not as good as some but that takes us into the realm of bogie design and the track-bed which is beyond the bounds of this chapter. In this respect, Eastleigh and Lancing, the main carriage works of the Southern, seemed to be denied the knowledge which enabled Wolverton (LNWR) and Derby to produce such smoothly running coaches. However, it should be mentioned that far and away the most comfortably riding coaches of the Southern Electric trains in the late 1920s were some converted all-third class coaches of the old LBSCR which were used in pairs to increase to eight vehicles the new three coach sets of 1925. They were otherwise spartan things with hard seats and you were squashed nine compartments to the coach but the bogies seemed so smooth that one imagined them to have been designed and built at Derby. The actual carriages must have been about 20 years old when I knew them.

In the 1930s the GWR made a bold move in carriage design with the production of rather splendid and exceptionally roomy corridor coaches for the 'Cornish Riviera Express'. By having doors only at the ends, and recessed, the bodies could be built out to the maximum width and the GWR loading gauge was exceptionally wide because it derived from the broad gauge days. Thus the space in tunnels and bridges was greater than normal on standard gauge lines. The extra dimensions must have given comfort to many a traveller sitting four-a-side in the corridor coaches at the height of the holiday season. Named the 'Centenary Riviera', these carriages commemorated the fact that the GWR was the only railway in Britain which had survived for one hundred years under the same name as that in which it was originally founded. All the others had suffered some change in the Grouping. Curiously enough that same line frequently produced at the rear end of its important expresses – though not on the

36. The LMS 'Coronation Scot' introduced in 1937, the year of the coronation of King George VI, was an interesting follow-on to the 'Silver Jubilee'. The West Coast express ran from Euston to Glasgow, 401½ miles, in 6½ hours including one stop at Carlisle, and it had to surmount the long climbs to the summits of Shap and of Beattock. The streamlined Pacific locomotives with their four cylinders, designed by Stanier, had a front end very similar to that of the GWR Kings but with a much larger boiler and firebox. The very striking train is shown here near Hatch End with the engine in its original livery of Prussian blue.

'Riviera' – a distinctly elderly coach, sometimes even one with a clerestory roof. This could be the first thing that struck the traveller as he approached his platform at Paddington: it would be the 'Slip'. It was carefully labelled with its prominent destination board and the tickets of all passengers were carefully scrutinised to make sure, for example, that the Plymouth passenger did not find himself 'slipped' off at Exeter. The practice was beginning to decline during the 1930s. Rising wages made it more expensive and there was reluctance to carry a second guard on the one train, especially if he had to be carried home 'on the cushions' (i.e. without working). However the GWR continued the practice longer than any other line and there was a certain entertaining element in it!

The year 1928 was notable for a long overdue advance in night journeys – the introduction of the third class sleeping car. True, it was a somewhat spartan design but for a modest supplement of a few shillings on the ordinary fare one had the exquisite comfort of being able to lie out flat. Based upon the ordinary third class corridor coach it provided four berths, two lower approximately where the ordinary seats would be, and two more above them. With a pillow and rug supplied there was tolerable comfort though lavatory accommodation had to be shared with the others at the end of the corridor. Forced ventilation seemed to keep the air fresh and the first time I tried one I slept totally without interruption from Holyhead to Euston where I awoke to the sound of the brakes going on. Of course one did not undress to any extent but ability to 'loosen the girths' all round gave one the chance to relax comfortably and not suffer the all-night misery of a bend in the tummy. For a family travelling to Scotland with up to four children (who could 'top and tail') the third class sleeper was a revelation, though it was to be another 25 years before the thirds could enjoy a proper berth with sheets on it and the possibility of changing into night clothes.

Having touched upon all but one of the major improvements in carriages between the wars it is perhaps appropriate to mention some of the bad old features which were rapidly disappearing and which were certainly not being perpetuated in the new construction. For a start, all new coaches were mounted upon bogies, there was no more of the hard running of four or six wheels which for some years after the war of 1914 had still been the lot of the suburban or rural branch line traveller. Also steam heating could be taken for granted in the late 1920s. There had been some rather meanly designed six-wheelers with no hot pipes beneath their seats which nevertheless displayed beside their couplings the flexible pipes through which the steam could pass from the adjoining vehicle. But, alas, the steam went straight through, under the body of the coach and on to its neighbour to warm the rest of the train. A knowledgeable traveller could have been sorely disappointed, after observing the whiffs of steam fore and aft of the old six-wheeler, to find that he had still to generate his own heat for the journey.

The other defect from earlier days was gas lighting. Though electric lighting for trains had been used since the turn of the century there was still a very large amount of gas in use throughout the 1914 war. Many of the old coaches dug out from sidings to make up the scores of troop specials would have been gas-lit and it was old Great Central stock of this kind, into which the soldiers were locked at the start of the journey, which was involved in the fire and the appalling death roll after the Quintinshill triple collision on the Caledonian Railway in 1915. Until well into our period the legacy of the Midland still left its mark with its small engine policy and reluctance to move on to electric lighting – which placed an additional burden upon the engine.

What seemed at the time an interesting technical advance of the 1930s was the extended use of the Gresley system of 'articulated' carriages, by which two vehicles were mounted upon three bogies by the simple expedient of having the inner ends, as it were, sharing the one bogie. Previously it had been used for the three-coach dining sets with the kitchen in the middle. In that case it was four bogies which supported the three vehicles, whereas the conventional arrangement would have needed six bogies. The principal had also been applied to some of the LNER suburban sets. It was carried further with the famous high speed train produced by Gresley for the 'Silver Jubilee' express running non-stop between Kings Cross and Newcastle in four hours.

The weight of the special streamlined seven-coach train was appreciably lightened by the reduction in the number of bogies and this assisted the continuous running at 75 to 90 mph. It was a very fine and enterprising effort, the train being named in commemoration of the 25-year reign of King George V, and it demonstrated that another contemporary locomotive design was far in advance of the pre-war standards. The principle of articulation which ensured a smoother ride was not developed further and used by any other railway, presumably because of the added complexity of having to use such coaches always in sets of two and three at a time, and their costs were higher.

All in all it can safely be said that the railway carriage at all levels, whether on crack express, semi-fast train or branch line was, in 1939, much more comfortable and likely to be a good deal cleaner than it had been in 1920.

4
Railway Ships

In an island country like Britain it is inevitable that many of the railways end at the coast. Before the aeroplane the ship was the only means of travel to other countries so that railways inevitably went into the business of shipping. They either bought up existing vessels in the early days or built their own, frequently in association with the railway of the foreign country concerned. From the paddle steamers of the early nineteenth century the typical railway ship had developed to the twin screw vessels of the 1890s capable of a speed of 20 knots. Then came the first turbine driven ships in the early 1900s including the 'Princess Elisabeth' owned by the Belgian Government: a triple screw turbine ship of 1,747 tons capable of 24 knots on the long crossing from Dover to Ostend. Into the mid-1920s size and power steadily increased exceeding 2,000 tons in 1915 with the 'Biarritz' of the SE & CR company, and that size became more or less general after the first war. The Channel crossing remained, however, something dreaded by thousands of travellers if the sea was at all rough. Higher speeds produced by more sophisticated turbine propulsion in no way reduced the extent of pitching and rolling inescapable with a relatively small narrow ship in the choppy cross-seas of the Channel. For the hopelessly bad sailor the only place was down below, reclining with a basin at hand, surrounded by other sufferers (whose proximity

was, to say the least, depressing). A large proportion of travellers would be able to survive if they remained still, kept warm and got fresh air. This meant remaining on deck, delightful on a fine and calm day but a chilling and probably spray-covered ordeal if it were at all rough. Seasoned travellers who had sailed over Atlantic and Pacific oceans without a qualm and who scoffed at the very idea of *mal de mer* could find themselves totally incapacitated by one hour of 'open sea passage' from Dover to Calais.

The great need in the 1920s, apart from the stabiliser which was twenty years ahead, was for the shelter (or awning) deck where you could sit on an upholstered seat, watch the sea – if so minded – and be protected from the full force of wind and wave but not suffer the unpleasant fug which years ago seemed inescapable 'below'.

37. 'Wagons-Lits Paris–Londres par Ferry-Boat'. The very attractive and widely shown poster by which the Chemin de Fer du Nord and the Southern advertised their luxurious Dover–Dunkerque train-ferry service. Wagons-Lits coaches in their familiar blue livery were specially built to fit the reduced loading gauge of England but their general appearance was very close to that of the 'Blue Train'. They left Victoria and Paris Gare du Nord late in the evening, were shunted onto one of the two train ferries and taken off, after the crossing, in the small hours. The destination was reached at about 9.30 am and offered the most comfortable, if not the speediest, way of crossing the Channel. It was the route always preferred by the Duke and Duchess of Windsor. The Night Ferry train was exceptionally heavy and was one of the very few to be regularly double-headed on the Southern, when coming up from Dover with restaurant car in the morning.

51

38. The Ostend steamer, 'Prinz Leopold', leaving Dover in 1931. Though a modern ship (2900 tons) in her day, more than half of her main deck is without any side protection from the sea – nice enough on a warm day but cheerless for even an hour's crossing through much of the year. Most Channel ferries of the time were similar.

The Southern made an assault on this problem with their two new ships 'Maid of Kent' and 'Isle of Thanet', each of 2,700 tons, in 1925 and in the 'Canterbury' which was slightly larger and capable of 25 knots. This latter ship was produced especially for the de luxe Golden Arrow service introduced in 1929. That year, though it saw the devastating Wall Street crash and financial panic which heralded the great American depression, was nevertheless a peak year for the cross-Channel traffic. Air services were nibbling at it but could not compete in terms of real comfort with rail and ship, so that an all first class ship would have been seen as an excellent investment. The immediate point here is that the 'Canterbury' provided this all-enclosed passenger accommodation which for so long had been badly needed. Once adopted it became a feature of all future ships and removed much of the discomfort from all but the roughest crossings. Meanwhile there were plenty of the older ships in service with much of their accommodation out on the open deck. On an evening journey to Switzerland in January 1931 I remember sitting on deck in a crowded ship while spray lashed continually against the canvas side-screens which had been rigged between the rail and the deck above. It was very rough and stewards were busy handing out empty basins and removing full ones while passengers huddled in their overcoats and rugs. Many years before effective sea-sick remedies were in general use, and before passenger ships were equipped with stabilisers, conditions on

LCGB
(Ken Nunn Collection)

39. The Southern's 'Canterbury' (also 2900 tons) had entered service in 1929 for the de luxe 'Golden Arrow' service with its Pullman trains on both sides of the channel. It will be noticed at once that the fully decked-in space extends for the whole length of the passenger accommodation, though you could still sit on the open top deck among the life-boats if you wished. The great improvement was the provision of comfortable upholstered seats with large windows giving one a view of the sea but without having to face the full rigours of the climate. Later, most other Channel ferries followed this style.

the typical Channel steamer could be excessively unpleasant.

The advent of the enclosed, but well-ventilated and comfortable seating accommodation, as pioneered by the 'Canterbury', was a tremendous advance. To complete the picture of luxury in the 1930s one must mention that she was furnished with a 'Palm Court' in the stern, again all enclosed with a splendid view of the sea and with real palms set in great pots as well as pretty baskets of flowers suspended from the roof. It was all very much in keeping with the highest standards of the period. For those wanting privacy and still more luxury there were a number of private cabins. The final touch in this Golden Arrow service, besides the Pullman trains on both sides of the Channel, was the speed-up in the Customs examination: on the outward journey the officials travelled with the train from Calais to Paris, examining the luggage while the train was running, and on the return the Golden Arrow passengers were segregated at Dover and given priority through Customs so that the train could be dispatched as quickly as possible. Thus the journey time from Paris to London was cut to 6½ hours and this first class all-Pullman journey was to be had for 5 pounds inclusive. That year of 1929 was the peak of pre-war Channel crossings with 1,109,000 passengers; in 1931 when England went off the gold standard and the £ was devalued, the numbers were halved.

40. Dover Marine Station from which one passed direct from the Boat Train to the waiting steamer ('Aux Bateaux' the Nation railway kindly informed the passengers at the end of the platform). The train shown here is an early all-Pullman though Museu not the 'Golden Arrow'. The rather handsome loco is one of the SECR E1 4–4–0 type re-built by Maunsell from Wainwright's 1905 design. Its regular run between London and Dover was no more than seventy miles but stiff gradients and sharp curves called for hard work.

That so-called 'shelter deck' on the 'Canterbury' led the way for all future ordinary accommodation on the new ships and is still to be seen in most if not all car ferries, including even the small steamers which ply to the Isle of Wight and in the Clyde estuary.

Meanwhile the LNER was developing the former GER service from Harwich to the Hook of Holland. For many years it had been extremely convenient for travellers to Holland, Switzerland and to all parts of Germany, the sea crossing being done at night on steamers well provided with single-berth cabins. To develop further what was then advertised as the 'business man's route to the Continent' three splendid new ships, the 'Prague', the 'Vienna' and the 'Amsterdam' were built. Each of 4,000 tons, they were like young liners, accommodating 450 first class in their separate cabins, and of course offering good restaurants for those who preferred not to take their dinner or breakfast on either of the connecting trains in Holland or England.

Apart from two large motor ships put on to the Dover–Ostend run by the Belgian Government in the 1930s, all these vessels were powered by steam driven turbines. Steam was still the means of propulsion for the many rather pretty looking paddle steamers which served the Isle of Wight and the Clyde. It was not until after the Second World War that the labour-saving diesel engine became all but universal on most small ships with the heavy thud of its exhaust and the somewhat pervasive smell of its oil. As upon railways the period was still one which was almost entirely dependent upon steam though oil-firing of the boilers was normal by then. It is curious to reflect that, while in modern ships the back-breaking labour of stoking by hand was no more, even the latest steam locomotives were to demand it until the end of the steam era in the 1960s. The automatic coal firing devices for locomotives which worked successfully in USA and elsewhere never developed beyond the trial stage here.

While captaincy of a cross-Channel steamer might be thought of as no more than a routine job, it called, nevertheless, for an extremely high standard of seamanship. Across one of the busiest sea-ways in the world with vessels of all sizes constantly sailing at right angles to the direction of the railway ship, where the weather is notoriously uncertain and subject to rapid changes, the captain must pick his way. He is running to an exact timetable, conscious that every minute lost must be accounted for and, subject to the over-riding need for safety, he must keep up a good speed. Then at each port he must bring his vessel in through a narrow entrance and alongside the quay with the utmost precision – and usually without the assistance of a tug. The fact that one so very rarely heard of accidents of any kind to such ships – even before the days of radar – is tribute to the excellence of their navigation and management.

There were more than a score of ships ranging from the little paddle steamers, still being built between the wars, up to the fine vessels like small liners which connected Britain with its neighbouring islands and various continental countries. At one time besides the normal sailings from Dover, Folkestone, Southampton and Portsmouth, there were curiosities like the night run from Tilbury to Dunkirk (a real poor man's route this: I went on the cheap for a French holiday most successfully one year, dozing in a chair on deck through the summer night). Then there were the routes to Ireland from Fishguard, Holyhead, Liverpool and Fleetwood.

The Scots had also pride of their own in the little fleet of paddle steamers which served the Clyde estuary and the routes to the islands from Oban. These ships were run by the railways and before 1923 they were painted in different colours according to whether they were the property of the Caledonian, the Glasgow & South Western, or maybe the North British Railway. It used to be a matter of local pride for the traveller to be able to identify by the colour of its funnel, the railway to which the steamer belonged. They had a tradition of smartness and cleanliness which was well maintained after the Grouping in 1923 and the LMS and LNER between them ran these routes (assisted in some parts by ships of the McBrane Line).

5
How It Was

What did it all look like in those twenty years? How did the scene change and what were the big differences between the world of railways then and now? In spite of the great advance of electrification in one or two parts of the country it was still most decidedly a steam era. It is easy to think today that too much emphasis went into its observation and into the description of steam locomotives but the fact remains that in the 1930s without steam the transport system of Great Britain would have collapsed. There was something enormously impressive about the great billowing clouds of the stuff which were inseparable from the steam-drawn train. 'Water-vapour' our physics masters might call it – true steam being invisible – but the world knew it as 'steam'. Whether going up in great separate puffs at the start of the journey or bursting out from a tunnel mouth or rolling off across a field on a side wind, this prodigal outpouring of pure white smoke looked wonderful. Only in the middle of a heat wave in high summer did it become invisible and only at the moment of a shovelful of coal being shot into the fire did the smoke blacken momentarily. W. H. Auden caught it beautifully with his 'Shovelling white steam over her shoulder' of the engine in early morning, in the poem *Night Mail* accompanying the documentary film of that title. Anyway there was steam! It may have contained those tiny particles of unburnt coal and it left dirt behind it, especially on the glass roof of a station, but it was an unforgettable feature along with the warm colours of most of the locomotives of the period.

Another feature of the scene was the comparative formality and 'respectability' of the average crowd seen to be travelling by train. That nearly all commuters should travel to their work wearing a hat and gloves, all the year round, was taken for granted and indeed many employers such as the banks would disapprove

41. A GWR delivery lorry of the 1920s, solid-tyred and very high above ground, but smartly turned out. It is interesting to see how small a proportion of the vehicle could be used for carrying goods (but the Publicity Department of the GWR made sure that its services were made widely known).

British Rail

56

42. 'The Torbay Limited', the second most popular holiday train of the GWR, prepares to leave Paddington in the 1920s. The cloche hat is worn by smart ladies and no gentleman is hatless! The senior ticket collector is resplendent in frock-coat and stiff collar and, as ever on the GWR, the carriages are boldly labelled at roof level.

of less. It is interesting, however, to see from a photograph in the *Railway Magazine* how the crowds queueing for a day excursion at Waterloo are dressed. They are going to Southampton on a trip to see over the RMS *Berengaria* (formerly the German liner *Imperator*), one of the most famous Cunarders until the launch of the *Queen Mary*. It is a day out for everyone but not a bare head can be seen and every male has a collar and tie – no open neck shirts in 1929. The trip, incidentally, was a bright piece of Southern enterprise: the crowds were so great that six trains had to be run in place of the single one planned and only a tank engine could be found for the last train. This, designed for short journeys, was obliged to stop twice for water. For thousands who would be unlikely, in those days, ever to sail in a big ship the opportunity to see over a great liner – kitchens and all – was irresistible.

Long distance excursions were immensely popular and, unlike those of pre-1914 trains, consisted usually of corridor stock and ran at express speeds. Best value of all perhaps were the 25 shilling (£1·25) trips of the LNER to Edinburgh to see the Rugger Internationals – up on the Friday about 10.00 p.m. from King's Cross to arrive Waverley 6.30 a.m. and back that night to reach London about 6.30 a.m. on the Sunday morning. (Most interesting for a Southerner, the first time, to see the North Eastern Atlantic come on at York.) It was all quite decorous in those days; in side-corridor coaches one travelled peacefully and mothers, cousins and aunts could safely be taken along for the ride to visit Scottish relatives. The LMS was

43. The 'Cornish Riviera Express' in full splendour, drawn by the four cylinder Star class engine, 'Reading Abbey', which is steaming well through the spacious cutting at Twyford. Sunshine gleams on her boiler and cylinder-top and all the carriages seem immaculately clean even though they have doubtless come up the 226 miles from Plymouth the previous day. The dining car, fourth from the front, goes right through to Penzance, but several coaches at the end of the train will be slipped off *en route*. Note that characteristic steep inclination of the GWR signals in the 'off' position. *Real Ph*

44. Solid comfort in a first-class dining car of the GWR's 'Cornish Riviera Express' in 1929. Every passenger has the satisfaction of a snow-white antimacassar against which to lean the head, the high seat-backs give a nice sense of privacy, and after dark the table lamps can confer a certain intimacy while a good four-course meal is consumed. The 'Buffy' car with its self-service snacks, its cardboard plates and plastic cups is still far off!

British Rail

equally good about Ireland, and for the same price, though here one travelled on the 'Irish Mail' 8.45 p.m. from Euston crossing on the boat from Holyhead at around 2 a.m. A useful amount of sleep could be had on both train and ship, while a Dublin breakfast could be memorable.

Though grouped, the railways were still privately owned and showed considerable enterprise in exploiting their services for more than 'straight' travel from one point to another. For those who regarded first class train travel as the method *par excellence* of moving around – and seeing – the country effortlessly, the seven day tour of Scotland from King's Cross was another magnificent idea of the LNER. For £20 all-in you were conveyed by first-class sleeper to Edinburgh where you had a day of sightseeing, then on, during the next night, to Aberdeen. More trips there, then they worked their way

45. A GWR local train at Norton Fitzwarren in 1930. The front carriage is evidently a through coach judging by its headboard; it has probably been detached from an express at Taunton and is now heading for Barnstaple. The double frames and external side-rods of the 4–4–0 loco, also its outside bogie springs and bearings, convey the flavour of an earlier GWR.

Rail Archive Stephenson

back via the Highlands, West Coast and finally Melrose before returning to Edinburgh for the last night journey home to London. Two sleeping cars accommodated the passengers and a third one the quite extensive staff who travelled with them. There were two dining cars and ordinary coaches for daytime travel, so it is not surprising that over the Scottish lines two engines were needed because it was a heavy train. It was well patronised at the time, though probably became less profitable as costs and wages rose and wider car ownership became more general.

Mention of staff reminds one of the lavish profusion of agreeable stewards, waiters and attendants who seemed to be about then. At the top level there was the unhurried, leisurely serving of lunch from Euston with a minimum three hours of journey ahead preceded with the offer of a drink directly you sat down. While at the other extremity the Southern on its newly electrified Portsmouth line would achieve a freshly made pot of tea and toast on the 30-mile dash down to Guildford – and all for ninepence. Another effort at service was the provision on Friday evenings in summer, on the busy 5.50 train from Waterloo, of an extra restaurant car set solely for the sale of drinks to the thirsty

46. The 'Cheltenham Flyer', 'the world's fastest train', tearing through Slough station at 80 mph on 26 April 1934. The four-cylinder Castle 4–6–0 appears to be no. 111, 'Viscount Churchill'. It was the day of the five hundredth run of the train. The branch line to Windsor and Eton diverges to the left of the photo.

travellers of the stockbroker belt – the extra facility closed down after Haslemere and the barman left the train.

The old Great Eastern Railway had looked after its season-ticket holders well especially those from Clacton and Walton-on-the-Naze, and in the 1930s the LNER saw to it that a large restaurant car, of Great Northern pattern, should cater for those who would breakfast on the early train. So, at Arnold Bennett's old station, Thorpe-le-Soken, in came, from Clacton, behind a fine new Gresley type of 4–6–0, this welcome breakfast car to which the Walton portion was attached. Never did bacon and eggs taste better as one spun up the estuary of the river Colne round the sweeping curves to Colchester – no self-service nonsense then in a

'Buffy' car for the meal was served to you at the table (alongside ·the fine long window) and, a pleasant feature, the marmalade was presented *not* as thin jelly in a miniature pot, but as a whole one-pound pot set in a splendid electro-plated container which insulated you totally from any stickiness. And so, I fancy, was the method of serving marmalade all over the four Groups and breakfast was ever one of their very best meals.

Appearance still counted for much and in days when the wearing of some sort of uniform was not seen as unduly servile but rather as proof of a natural pride in the job, the general smartness of railway servants was most noticeable. It ran down all the way from the top stationmasters, a title which sounded so much more impressive than the Station Manager of today. In the 1920s

47. Described in 1928 by the LMS as 'semi-open first class', this carriage could of course be coupled to a kitchen car and used as a diner. Its seats were very comfortable and amply provided with antimacassars for all. The upholstery was very fine and luxurious, but the ornate roof lights and the table lamps were neither of them ideal for reading, unless you bent forward over the table.

48. The 1935 version of the same LMS vehicle. No antimacassars and a rather tasteless pattern for the fabric of the upholstery, but they let themselves go on the woodwork with some quite impressive graining. Unfortunately fashions of the time dictated the ugly box-like fixtures for lighting and the clumping brackets for luggage racks.

the stationmaster at Crewe, for example, looked every inch the man in charge of the most famous station on the Premier Line (though it was then part of the LMS). He wore a morning coat, sported a carnation in his buttonhole, he had the ends of his moustache waxed and he wore a silk hat. It somehow gave the finishing touch to learn that he had spent the whole of his railway life at Crewe starting in 1887 on the lowly duties of ground pointsman. There was no doubt that behind the well turned out, almost dandified figure there was a railwayman through and through.

The 'appearance' principle was very marked also in such items as Pullman cars. All the first class ones bore names and one, 'Princess Patricia', greatly cared for by the Southern, was refurbished with handsome upholstery, inlaid panelling (very much of the period), a larger

kitchen and was then specially allocated to the important 8.45 a.m. up from Brighton to London Bridge – a real stockbrokers' express – and the 5 p.m. down. On Saturdays it was switched to Victoria and served the 1 p.m. to Brighton for the weekenders. Its seats and its bogies were no better sprung than average but the *look* of the thing attracted customers – and of course the Pullman attendants in their smart uniforms helped greatly.

Turning again to some of the actual trains: the newspaper specials, run at express speeds from London in the early hours, were exciting and could be useful for the passenger. The one which suited me for joining my family in North Cornwall after they had begun the holiday earlier, was the 1.25 a.m. from Waterloo. Besides the several vans loaded with newspapers delivered at the last moment from Fleet Street,

H. C. Casserley

49. LSWR Adams Jubilee 0–4–2 no. 602, built in 1894, still going strong in Southern livery in 1931, on a Portsmouth train just approaching Clapham Junction. The ten-coach load of main-line stock is quite considerable but the train would probably divide at Woking, part going to Alton. The second coach is a LSWR speciality: originally a three-class composite plus guard's van, it also had lavatory access for every compartment (though it had no corridor). It was designed especially as a through carriage which could be detached at, say, Sidmouth Junction and then coupled to the branch-line train to be worked down to the resort. On the right of the photo can be seen the remains of the recently abandoned overhead electrification of the LBSCR.

50. The celebrated 'Brighton Belle' all-Pullman express, one of the best-looking third-rail electric trains ever to run. For over thirty years it was greatly loved by its regular patrons, many of whom were commuters, and when the Pullman train was withdrawn some years ago it was mourned by several distinguished people in the columns of 'The Times'. Made up normally of two six-coach sets, the first and last coach in each set carried the traction motors on both its bogies and did not therefore run very smoothly. Nevertheless the train had an engaging character of its own with smartly uniformed attendants waiting at the terminus at each of the end doorways, and on the journey ready to serve refreshments, early and late in the day, to every seat in the train. It was a splendid flagship for the Southern, for the Pullman Car Company and for the famous resort of Brighton.

LCGB (Ken Nunn Collection)

Rail Archive Stephenson

51. Southern Railway four-cylinder ex-LSWR 4–6–0 in the pleasantly wooded – and in April primrose-covered – cutting on the London side of Surbiton station. Nicknamed the 'paddle-boats' because of their huge splashers over the coupled wheels, these engines with their high-pitched boilers and handsome chimneys looked impressive; they could run very fast but their performance was sometimes uncertain as they required exceptional skill in firing. Here no. 460 is on a Portsmouth express of ancient, partly gas-lit, non-corridor stock, all too common for a seventy-mile run in 1926. The headcode indicates that the train must slow down shortly to take a cross-over at Hampton Court Junction for the Cobham line down to Guildford.

there were just a few ordinary side-corridor coaches and if you had the side to yourself you could travel very comfortably. The train, drawn by the latest 4–6–0, rushed down the empty track with only two stops to Exeter. There the train split up at about 5 a.m. and I recall an obliging porter at Okehampton who would fill my mug with boiling water so that I could shave in comfort while the train waited there. The GWR, too, had a good newspaper flier which did Taunton non-stop from Paddington, 143 miles in 150 minutes, while the LMS carried the London news up to Inverness faster than the 'Royal Highlander', their best sleeping car express.

As an indication of the light-hearted attitude towards smoking – lung cancer then unsuspected by the public – there was a move towards increasing the proportion of smoking compartments to 70 per cent of the accommodation, where earlier on most lines it had been less than 50 per cent. Worse still, for non-smokers, it was

52. An Adams 4–4–2 tank engine of the 1880s taken into Southern branch-line service when over forty years old. It is seen in 1925 at Axminster station in beautiful condition, about to set off on the Lyme Regis branch. Three engines of the class remained until the 1950s because their exceptionally light axle-loading and bogies enabled them to negotiate the sharp curves of that branch line more easily than could the Drummond 0–4–4 tanks.

only *their* compartments which were marked; it was assumed that everywhere one could smoke unless the triangular sign of NO SMOKING was on the windows.

A great social advance was the increase in the number of people who had holidays with pay: as wage earners the bulk of them ceased work on the Friday evening and wished to travel on the Saturday. In those days seaside landladies catered for the vast majority of holiday-makers and they had to make their bookings from Saturday to Saturday so that day became the

inescapable one for the journey. Besides the 'Summer Timetable' of most railways there was the great spread of 'Saturdays only' trains. Often run as duplicates or triplicates of ordinary trains, they were not unduly crowded and gave many people a quite comfortable journey (including sometimes a special cheap family two-course lunch for 2s 6d (12½p)). The Saturday workings of a railway could become a fascinating study for the enthusiast, beginning with the sight, on Friday evenings, of sidings 12 miles or more from the terminus stuffed full with the extra

53. The LNER down 'Clacton Pullman' toiling up Brentwood Bank in 1930. The engine is a pre-1914 Holden 4–6–0 but it seems to be in an exemplary state with every detail of its livery, lettering and bright work apparently spotless, the original Prussian blue of the GER replaced by LNER (ex-GNR) green. They were always fine-looking engines and, although not of high tractive effort, they regularly kept time with the heavy 'Hook Continental Express' and the well-loaded Norfolk coast holiday trains.

54. LNER Pacific in action on a Leeds express near Hadley Wood. The engine is steaming well and blowing off slightly despite the long climb from King's Cross. A scene of the early 'thirties, it is typical that the leading coach should be an elderly wooden-bodied clerestoried survivor of pre-1914 days.

Rail Archive Stephenson

"THE CORONATION"
ON THE EAST COAST ENTERING SCOTLAND
IT'S QUICKER BY RAIL
FULL INFORMATION FROM ANY L·N·E·R OFFICE OR AGENCY

FRANK H. MASON

55. A good specimen of one of the many excellent railway posters of the 1930s: this shows the LNER 'Coronation' express on its six-hour journey over the more level East Coast route. Besides the streamlining they now went in for a beaver-tailed observation car at the rear. It is depicted at a dramatic point where the line runs at the edge of the Northumberland coast north of Berwick. Bamburgh Castle and the Farne Islands are in the

LCGB (Ken Nunn Collection)

56. The Royal Train of the LNER travelling from Wolferton (for Sandringham) to King's Cross in 1938 and seen near Potters Bar. The ex-GER 4–4–0 of the Claud Hamilton class shows the traditional four-disc (or lamp) headcode for royalty. These engines, built in 1900, were first re-built with the Belpaire firebox and later superheated with an extended smokebox. The well-polished steel ring in the smokebox door was always a striking feature of them in the inter-war period.

trains waiting to be taken into the terminus on the Saturday morning. Then one would see dear old veteran engines brought back from retirement, to make a sprightly run to the sea and back.

The new travelling public took less luggage with them and more often carried it themselves in bulging suitcases which filled up the compartment while the guards' vans remained almost empty. At one time the absurdities of trousers which could measure 32 inches at the foot – and the comic, but fetching little 'po' hats of the girls, pulled down over their eyes, added fun to the travel scene.

Meanwhile the railways had another feature – the camping coach. This was an ingenious use of otherwise superannuated coaches, mostly six-wheelers, which were fitted up with bunks, tables and all reasonable camping equipment, painted up attractively and then settled (with brakes firmly on and wheels chocked!) in a siding at some little station in a beautiful part of the country. They cropped up all over the railways and were very popular. Nearness to the station ensured their water supply and other vital services.

6
Stations and Signals

The start of our period found most railway stations little changed from the early years of the century. Very few indeed of the great termini had been rebuilt apart from Waterloo and Victoria, most stations of any size had grown piecemeal with the odd extra platform, or bay, tacked on as needed. Between the wars

57. Below the fine symmetry of Brunel's beautiful roof to Paddington station stands the 1930 tea trolley. The train looks suspiciously empty and the photograph has probably been posed, but it gives a faithful reminder of the trolley service, which within its limits was good. 'Light lunch boxes with sandwiches, cake and fruit 1/–' (5p) was good value and apples and chocolate were also on offer. A nice cup of tea was to be had, freshly made in a pot. As usual the refreshments man is well turned out in a smart peaked cap and wearing his waistcoat.

British Rail

there seemed to be an effort to re-plan at many places and build again to suit the precise needs of traffic which had grown so enormously in the past 20 years.

Partly because of its electrification and increased train service the Southern was particularly active over stations. The concrete buildings of its new stations looked bare and unfriendly to some eyes but they were efficient. The hundreds of 'regulars' using Surbiton station, for example, mourned the passing of their nice old wooden stairs leading to the middle platform for fast trains and their ability to run straight in on to the outer platforms for local trains. At first the concrete stairs of the new station were hated and *all* were obliged to use them because the four lines were served by the two faces of two island platforms. If an incoming train were unexpectedly switched from local to the through line it was in fact much simpler just to cross from one side to the other of the platform rather than be obliged to run up and down two flights of steps. Woking and Wimbledon, two other busy stations, were transformed from cosy – some would say cramped – wooden buildings into large windy concrete expanses and, in order to help drivers to spot their signals more easily the bridges were made higher above the line. Older travellers complained at the extra number of steps to be climbed while younger railway lovers were

58. Victorian railway architecture standing up well in 1936. Ely station, built originally by the GER and now part of the LNER. As in so many railway stations, the basic engineer's approach to the problem seemed to produce a clean, straightforward building which had symmetry and genuine fitness-for-purpose. Here there is ample cover for passengers waiting for their train, room is provided for all the ancillary services and it looks good.

British Rail

deprived of that delicious whoosh of steam which used to shoot up from a passing train between the boards of the old wooden bridges. The new stations were, of course, more efficient and had some good clean lines in their very 1930-ish architecture but they lost character. As they were rebuilt they seemed all to look alike.

For some strange reason when the LSWR built Woking station in Victorian times they provided no platform for the up through line of the four tracks. It was an important and growing place where many semi-fast trains stopped increasingly and if approaching on the fast line they had to take a cross-over, just outside the station, to bring them to this one platform. To see a train neatly snaking its way across from one line to the other was peculiarly satisfying and it was likely to be switched back on to the fast line after Woking for a non-stop run to Waterloo. At busy times such as early evening, trains

59. Crewe, one of the busiest and most famous stations in the country, at a time of transition. The LNWR type of semaphore signal, with its somewhat short 'slotted' arm and the flat top to the signal post, is shortly to be replaced by all-light signals controlled electrically. In the upper centre of the photo is an example of the 'theatre-light' system where the five bulbs set in diagonal formation will light up to indicate that a train has to take points to the right after it has been given the go-ahead from the light below. The cross surmounting the electric signal lights indicates that the new system is not yet in operation. Such a scene was common in many parts at that time as the railways prepared to modernise their signalling.

Other characteristics of the Crewe scene are the massive battery of signals on the huge gantry in the distance and the awning above the platform to the right with its typical LNWR style of saw-tooth roof, solid and enduring. A Royal Scot locomotive, with its diminutive chimney on the huge boiler, hovers on the right in the distance beyond the platform.

from Salisbury, Bournemouth and Portsmouth might all converge on Woking in a short time and, having to make a stop there, you often saw one held impatiently at a signal in 'Woking yard' while the train ahead was still standing at the platform; in the pre-electric era that meant the pushing out from a siding of the earlier Alton portion of the train and coupling it to the Portsmouth one – all at that one platform. Most interesting for the watcher – 'something always happening at Woking' you thought, but it was a potential nightmare for signalmen, especially as the through line at that point was a regular 70 mph section for expresses. To their credit, in those days of mechanical signal working, long

before the sophisticated all-electric systems of today, there never seemed to be any accidents there.

So, Woking was equipped with its fourth platform for the up through line and became much more efficient but less interesting. The same thing happened at Exeter Queen Street, too, (now Central) was rebuilt and lost its old-fashioned but imposing all-over wooden roof. It was given much longer platforms, a great advantage for the division and making-up of trains which occurred there frequently in Southern days and before the line had been handed over to the Western, after nationalisation.

60. Harrow-on-the-Hill, Metropolitan, a good example of a modern suburban station in the 1930s style. Rounded edges to the platform awnings and steel-framed windows are much in fashion, while concrete is used wherever possible, as for the name-boards and lamp standards. Overall there is general neatness and tidiness which show some advance.

Other Groups, though they were not then preparing for electrification, made great improvements to many of their stations. The GWR was especially active in South Wales where new stations were built at Newport, Cardiff and Swansea and the harbour at Fishguard was much improved. Among many other stations brought up to date was Taunton where another great all-over wooden roof, dating from Broad Gauge days, disappeared and four through-platforms took the place of the former two. On the LMS, Wembley Central and Luton were rebuilt but the totally new Euston was deferred until electrification in the 1960s. The LNER followed an architecturally more pleasing style than some

by use of a well chosen brown brick for many of their new stations of which Leeds Central and its new hotel were the most important. Good work was also done at some of the busier suburban stations of the old GER section.

Colour light signalling and electrically worked points transformed the handling of trains into and out of the great terminal stations and with provision of signals at more frequent intervals it was possible to run trains closer together and yet with a greater margin of safety. Also the powerful 'bull's eye' signal lights pierced fog more effectively than had been the case with the former oil lamps.

No one who remembers railway travel in fog

under the old conditions of semaphore signals, mechanically worked and supplemented by the fogmen in their little line-side huts – rather like sentry boxes – could fail to admire the work of the up-to-date signal engineer. Like most modern developments in railway equipment the special character, and for the enthusiast, much of the interest of the original forms of signalling disappeared. No longer was the magnificent cluster of signals to be seen massed upon a great gantry at an important junction – no more could the amateur enjoy trying to sort out from twenty or more signals which particular line they controlled and what message they conveyed to the driver.

It was, however, all brilliantly worked out with the main colours of green, red, yellow and double yellow plus the clever use of 'theatre lights' – a strip of white bulbs in line – at different angles to serve as direction indicators. Another idea, to which I became much attached, was at a terminus where the adaptation of a cluster of bulbs signalled the number of the platform into which you were going to run. Faintly neurotic perhaps but if you got a view of the number it saved useful time *not* to be bunched against a door on the wrong side of the train.

So the standards of signalling advanced in various places and on every Group. The LNER did much to safeguard their new high speed trains from the time of the 'Silver Jubilee' in 1935 onwards. At Darlington there was a new all-electric signal-box while on the York to Northallerton section provision was made for signals at 1,300-yard intervals to enable trains at 65 mph to follow each other with gaps of only 2½ minutes between each (with slower trains naturally the time between them had to be longer). One sensed a new deal in railway travel then on the LNER – not just a few glorious bursts of 80 as on other lines, but down their great long stretches of dead straight track,

behind a Gresley Pacific, you pounded on and on for mile after mile at a very steady 70 mph it seemed.

Across the Border, at Galashiels and Selkirk Junction colour light signals were installed and stretches of the LMS received the same treatment. A new race of signal maintenance men had to be trained for the fresh equipment but the saving in operation costs, eventually,. were impressive as more and more of the old mechanical signals were dismantled. In the past, the open wires, angle-joints and pulleys all had to be kept oiled and the elaborate signal posts, often 20 or 30 feet high had to be kept painted and their oil lamps constantly replenished, whereas in the new era the work was mainly confined to the skills of the electrician and his wiring. All in all the 1930s showed a great advance in rail safety as the more important parts of the signalling system were considerably safeguarded against snow and ice (though widespread use of points heaters had to wait for another generation). Another great benefit of these electrical developments was that the modern signal-box could be equipped with a complete illuminated wall diagram showing exactly the movements of any train in relation to the signals controlled by that box. No longer was the signalman obliged to check each train by direct observation out of his windows; the gain in fog or darkness was very great.

London's Underground, too, was making great progress during these years. The techniques of electric signalling owed much to early experiments on the District line and the Tubes but it was now the turn of the Underground Group to give attention to the rather awful problem of rush hour crowds at the busiest stations in central London. The early 1920s found a huge increase in the numbers – of both men and women – who poured into and out of London morning and evening. The first type of

61. Elm Park Underground station about 1930. A good example of the successful effort made by Frank Pick and his design staff to tidy up everything, eg. making advance provision for the sweet-shop in a neat inset and carefully guarding against damage to the woodwork below the windows of the booking office.

Underground station as it evolved before 1914 was proving hopelessly inadequate at busy points. Issuing tickets by hand and then queueing for the lifts was too slow, and the latter excessively uncomfortable as people crowded in from the rear upon those already in the lift. Then those who had waited further back in the crowd, just as they thought their turn had come to get in, would be told, 'On the next lift please' as the outer doors slammed in their faces.

Tube stations built before 1907 had been too early to use the powerful escalator. The pioneer station with the exciting 'moving staircase' was Earl's Court in 1911 and by 1915 escalators were installed at ten stations including Liverpool Street, Paddington, Oxford Circus and Baker Street. (To allay passengers' anxieties at the start a man with a wooden leg, named 'Bumper Harris', was employed for some weeks just to ride continually up and down the Earl's Court escalator in its early days.) During the 1920s, with great enterprise, the Underground rebuilt their busiest stations at Oxford Circus, Bank and Tottenham Court Road and, in 1928, Piccadilly Circus, providing escalators to all. Invariably, it called for major excavations immediately below street level, some obstructions in the actual roadway and the fearsome complexities of water mains, drainage and electricity and telephone wires to be re-sited but the jobs were done and travellers gained in each case a fine new circulating area, a forest of slot machines to speed up ticket purchase and then the smooth glide down one of the many sets of moving stairs. For 50 years it has all been taken for granted but it seemed a miracle at the time and was a great achievement for its builders and planners.

Meanwhile the actual tube lines were pushed right out into the suburbs, to Edgware and Cockfosters in the north and to Morden in the south, with Golders Green to Morden constituting much the longest railway tunnel in the world, far outstripping those under the Alps. Earth-moving machinery was still elementary and great bands of navvies were responsible for most of this work much of which had to be carried on below busy London streets.

Under the direction of Lord Ashfield, the Chairman, and Frank Pick, the Managing Director, of the Underground Group the closest attention was paid to design. In the early days of the General Omnibus Company Edward Johnston's display types had been used for station names and destination boards on buses. Then the Curwen Press was employed to design and print posters and most important of all, an inspired architect, Charles Holden, was retained for the design of all the new stations. They perfectly fulfilled Frank Pick's definition that an Underground station should be 'An inviting doorway in an architectural setting that cannot be missed by the casual pedestrian'. They stood out particularly well in the rather routine shopping areas of the newly built suburbs of the time. So it was that the fifth railway Group, combined in 1933 into the then London Passenger Transport Board, set a new standard in design for stations as well as rolling stock, one which excited admiration from Paris and New York as well as other capitals.

There was an important breakthrough in mechanical design at the end of our period when the '1938' stock was produced for the Morden line trains. In this, by raising the floor of the coaches two or three inches, it became possible to fit in the motors and switchgear underneath the vehicles. In all tube trains until then they had been mounted above the end bogies of the motor coaches and had thus eliminated the chance for any passenger accommodation at that point. There was some stubbing of toes on the slightly higher floors at first (and hats were sometimes bashed on the nearer roofs) but the new trains were soon accepted, especially for their quieter running and better acceleration.

7
End of a Great Era

The author passed from boyhood to his early 30s during the period described in this book and thus is inevitably prone to regard it as a golden age of railway achievement. Memory of those years is still vivid and nothing can dim the fact that it *was* the high noon of steam. True, electric haulage was making its impression. Good electric expresses were running punctually – if not very smoothly – to Brighton and to Portsmouth but even the Southern Railway (that weasel-word Region not then in use) was proud of its steam services to Exeter and Bournemouth; elsewhere steam was unassailable.

The cheapest Ford car could be bought for 100 pounds, so could the Morris Minor (equal to about 2,000 pounds today) but the shadow of near universal 'holidays-by-car' was still far off. At midday on summer Saturdays Waterloo was jammed with holiday makers, at Paddington every seat was probably booked on the 'Cornish Riviera', while crowded trains from Leeds and Manchester disgorged their thousands at Scarborough and Blackpool. Railways were still the accepted way of travelling unless you were in the favoured minority; the frequent need to run second and third portions of popular trains was often the clear evidence.

Nearly all the country's freight went by train and every station had its active goods yard. The trusty 0–6–0 goods engine, often at least 40 years old, handled most of this traffic, much of it in four-wheeled trucks with no continuous brake and at speeds of about 30 mph. Today, half a century later, most railway equipment is altogether superior and more sophisticated. The track is usually welded on main lines and so much smoother and quieter that it becomes difficult to estimate speed or to know one's whereabouts in the dark. Bogies are better designed and sprung while much signalling is electric; altogether railway operation is freed from many of its former problems – not least of them the (alas!) often temperamental steam locomotive, the vagaries of which could cause delays and sometimes accidents. One could argue that railways today, what is left of them, are technically better than they were in the 1920s but there was then – and up to 1939 – a certain magnificence about the best lines, with an all-round interest and variety which no longer exists.

For all that the Grouping had swallowed up the smaller lines the great main lines still left their individual mark. The Great Western never had changed seriously. Despite modernisation its strong 'family' characteristics remained: the tapering boilers, the proud copper-capped chimneys and the same chocolate and cream livery for the coaches. The LMS was the old LNWR and the Midland rolled into one, mostly with the colours of the latter but also with a fine dash of Swindon about the latest Stanier locomotives. The LNER was different from either with its grass-green engines and varnished teakfinish coaches: it was really the old GNR which had imposed itself upon the powerful and once prosperous NER with its former plum-red carriages and the North British with its greenish-brown engines. So there, allowing for the all-green Southern, were the four distinct lines and at many important exchange stations, be it Carlisle, York, Leicester or Exeter St Davids, there was always the unfailing interest of being able to spot the locomotives and rolling stock of a different Group. Better still, those with memories going back to about 1920 were able to identify original LNWR, MR, LSWR or SECR stock even though it had been painted over in the livery of the new Group.

No one could doubt that the railways of Britain advanced enormously in the period of the Grouping and great credit goes to the management of each Group, not only to the top men such as Josiah Stamp or Herbert A. Walker but to the Chief Mechanical Engineers who achieved a tremendous degree of modernisation in those 16 years between 1923 and 1939. In the relentless test of six years of war their works were not found wanting.

Index